THIS IS M
AUTOM
THIS IS SALES AUTOMATION!

*A Compact Guide to Putting Sales on
Autopilot for SME*

Tim Cortinovis

will any legal responsibility or blame be held against the publisher for any reparation, damages, or monetary loss due to the information herein, either directly or indirectly.

Respective authors own all copyrights not held by the publisher.

The information herein is offered for informational purposes solely and is universal as so. The presentation of the information is without contract or any type of guarantee assurance.

The trademarks that are used are without any consent, and the publication of the trademark is without permission or backing by the trademark owner. All trademarks and brands within this book are for clarifying purposes only and are owned by the owners themselves, not affiliated with this document.

First edition, 2020

ISBN: 979-8-5631700-8-7

To Stefanie. Thank you!

TABLE OF CONTENTS

Please do Not Tell Anyone Else

"There is one elementary truth, the ignorance of which kills countless ideas and splendid plans, that the moment one definitely commits oneself that Providence moves, too. Whatever you can do or dream you can do, begin it. Boldness has genius, power, and magic in it. **Begin it now.**"

— Johann Wolfgang von Goethe

You know what? Deep in my heart I am a lazy pig. Ever since I started working in b2b sales I thought 'How can I get myself out of the equation?' This was some 20 years ago, and since then I discovered a lot of tools, ideas and methods to automate tedious sales and marketing tasks.

Later on, when I became an entrepreneur, I noticed that these administrative and repetitive tasks were really the main obstacle holding me back from success. So I put even more emphasis on automating and scaling processes.

This helped me grow and scale. Nowadays, there are a lot of growth gurus promising the one and only recipe for massive growth. Of course, there are some hacks and shortcuts. But I sincerely believe that real and lasting growth comes from us as humans. With our ideas and sudden inspirations, and the necessary alignment with our goals, we can grow a company.

With ideas and automation together, nearly miracles can be done. Just take a closer look at "Blitzscaling". This does the magic also using automation.

How to use this book

My aim is to give you not only the needed background information on marketing and sales automation, but also the best practices I discovered over the years. I entitled them

1

"recipes" and you will find nine of them in the course of this book. All of them are practice-proven, also if you go short of manpower or budget.

What will you get?

A robust overview on the topic of sales and marketing automation, and some really hot hands-on recipes.

Salespeople and marketers do not like wasting time on boring, mundane activities in today's fast-paced environment. Automation will streamline processes for marketing. It will take care of today's top sales and marketers' goals. Therefore, it needs to be leveraged by organizations to minimize direct human interference and save time.

What makes a difference these days? Outstanding creativity in marketing and extreme customer centricity in sales. To get both, you crazily need automation, as with automation you can free your time and mind to be creative, and then match what your customers want.

Automation in marketing makes sense. This is now being found by many organizations to be real. By assessing what marketing automation is and examining the different advantages and benefits that these instruments offer, as well as understanding exactly why marketing automation strategies make sense for all industries, it is possible to see what can be achieved for these products.

Marketing automation for only a few companies is no longer an exclusive option. Its steady development and corporate assimilation has been remarkable, and this development at all levels of the distribution funnel tends to strengthen customer relationships. According to Gartner

CRM and customer experience software (with corresponding sales and marketing automation) it will continue to be among the fastest growing software segments.

Without the book you will discover a twofold way for the possible solutions. Whether you can apply a monolithic solution with one software product, or you can implement a variety of small and smallest tools to do the job.

Oftentimes we as SME entrepreneurs have to ensure not to exceed budgets. The wrong decision for a major digital tool may cost more than an arm and a leg. So, I think the best option is to choose some smaller tools. You will find many of them here.

And remember, it is not only important to reach the goals we have, but also to enjoy the ride. Stay tuned and have fun.

Part I: This is Marketing Automation!

Why

"I am happy when it rains. Because when I am not happy, it also rains."

- **Karl Valentin** (German humorist)

It is important to understand what marketing automation is and how it varies from CRM before getting underway. Marketing automation can be defined as software used to automate several marketing procedures, such as campaign management, customer segmentation, and customer data aggregation. It can also be used for lead incorporation, cross-selling and up-selling, increasing customer retention, marketing partnerships, and knowing the return on investment in marketing.

Marketing automation allows tasks to be completed more quickly, like other forms of automation. It sets up chances to carry out new kinds of techniques at about the same time. Marketing automation solutions reduce the amount of administrative activities that have to be carried out in the marketing department. It is possible to execute actions that have previously taken a lot of time even more quickly and effectively, freeing up marketing personnel to perform other activities. This ensures the marketing teams get more for their resources as they invest in an automation program, and it makes team members happier as they can use their time on creative tasks.

Organizations are often unclear about what marketing automation is, and they have it mixed with email marketing ways. Marketing automation differs from email marketing or the use of autoresponders for email, and it gives organizations a lot more.

Marketing automation is often confused with CRM; the two are different, though. CRM focuses on gathering knowledge relevant to current customer accounts and the driving of potential customer distribution pipelines.

However, marketing automation focuses on enhancing communication between leads at an early stage and scoring these to target energies appropriately, so the highest possible number of leads are converted into customers. CRM's overall objectives are arguably to help organizations better manage customer relationships and find ways to extend these. Marketing automation, however, has a different aim, which is to help advertisers develop their consumer targeting and strengthen connectivity with large leads. Marketing technology assists on a one-on-one basis with personalization and collaboration, and monitoring prospects do this. The two systems complement one another, and information can be synced between the two, which in turn has the excellent benefit of ensuring that there is consistency of the data and information the business stores about its customers.

By discovering what it is, we continue our search for the best marketing automation.

In order to optimize the campaign workflow, marketing automation refers to utilizing automated resources. Simply placed, it makes assignments more comfortable for you. It is doing so by the automation of routine activities such as emails, behavior on websites, Scheduling posts from social media, and measuring the efficiency of systems for marketing. This contributes to better organizational efficiency. It also helps grow sales.

In B2C firms, marketing automation has emerged as one of the main developments. Marketers now understand the value of automation and the need for it. Therefore, over the past few years, developments in marketing automation techniques have grown.

The automation software industry will expand at a rate of 8.55 percent, according to statistics. A market capitalization of about USD 16.87 billion is projected to be achieved by 2025.

More than 51 percent of organizations are using automation techniques. It also showed that 58% of B2B firms are planning on using it. So, for small businesses, you can imagine the growing need for automation.

Reasons to consider using Automation for Marketing.

It takes a little longer to introduce campaign automation, and most organizations won't see instant benefits. However, with persistence, marketing automation progress will help drive drastic results in many different areas for the brand.

How can Marketing Automation help your business?

- Increase in Productivity
- Generation of revenue
- Customer Retention
- Tracking and Measuring
- Gaining territory in the war of talents

Increase in Productivity

Around 74 percent of advertisers believe that time is saved by automation. This adds to efficiency optimization.

Generation of revenue

Other significant advantages of automation include an improvement in sales and lead conversion. Around 90 percent of organizations who employ these resources believe that their organization has gained. In comparison, B2C advertisers have seen conversion rates as high as 50 percent using these tactics.

Customer Retention

This is used by about 69 percent of B2B advertisers to get new buyers. Often, it is used by 50 percent of advertisers to attract them. It can offer substantial insights and predict their needs through their actions.

Tracking and Measuring

Data and analyses allow you to assess campaign success rates. You should then take the requisite steps based on these observations. Companies using these methods may track their content marketing campaigns three times more than those who do not use any monitoring or measuring.

Gaining territory in the war of talents

There is a lack of skilled experts, which is especially hard for SME. Automation helps in two ways to face the problem: First, it frees capacity within your teams, leveraging their creative abilities, and second, you are getting more attractive to applicants, as you can tell them that they are not going to do the tedious tasks. Recently I was in a workshop with some clients, all managing directors of large building suppliers. One of them stated "I would not get any applicant if I did not automate my sales and marketing processes.".

How to execute a plan for Marketing Automation?

1. Create interactive content
2. Project a campaign for a drip
3. Automate real-time teams

4. Using Follow-up Email Automation

5. Using automation in list segregation

For startups, mid-sized firms, and even corporations, there are several resources. However, without a substantial collection of elements, a successful approach is not complete.

These components will help you cook up a plan to simplify your small company, much like the Lasagna ingredients. For organizations of all types, these components are critical.

1. Create dynamic content

Build adaptive material that varies with the behavior of the recipients. 47 percent of consumers first read the web material before talking to a sales agent, a reported survey by DemandGenReport. Therefore, producing diverse content according to their desires is very necessary.

2. Plan a drip campaign

An automatic method that responsively sends emails over a period of time is a drip campaign. These promotions respond based on what the client wants, instead of sending the same material to all consumers. There is an 80 percent higher available rate and three times more click-through rates for drip campaigns.

3. Automate teams in real-time

The coordination distance between divisions is one of the greatest obstacles in any company. This brings inefficiency and a lack of teamwork. An electronic method of marketing guarantees fair access to all applicable consumer information.

As a benefit, it serves to minimize the ill consequences of the contact distance.

4. Use Email Automation for Follow-up

One of the main generators of revenue has been emailing marketing. It does so by delivering customized and guided emails to the leads. It is possible to pass a lead through multiple phases of the sales funnel. Automated follow-up and monitoring of replies are other significant advantages of email marketing. Studies indicate that the ROI can be as significant as $38 for the $1 email expense.

5. Use automation in list segregation

You will apply it to varied standards in order to segregate the clients. This helps to organize the lists properly and, depending on particular demands, target the plans.

What is the ROI on Automation of Marketing?

The next thing that comes to your mind is the budget and the ROI as you plan to simplify the processes. We would use scientific data in order to help you answer these questions.

To evaluate the correlation between investment and market results, McKinsey conducted a study. 82 % of respondents thought that the absence of automation made them inefficient. They said that the introduction of automation could provide a greater ROI. It can also boost marketing's contribution to overall business growth.

A second analysis by emailmonday.com showed that the money spent on marketing automation was beneficial for about 58 percent of respondents. 4 out of 5 consumers had improved lead generation, and greater conversions were seen by about 77 percent.

Consequently, we can confidently assume that there is no scam on marketing automation.

How much do Marketing Automation vendors charge?

Different vendor types and different software bundles exist. Both adhere to numerous consumer requirements. The distinction is in terms of pricing (leads, contacts, and subscribers) and contacts.

Low Tier Vendor: The price per year will range from $1200 to around $3000.

Middle Tier vendors: The rates start at about $12,000 in this segment, and go as high as $24,000 annually.

Top Tier Vendors: You can be paid about $45,000 a year and more by these vendors. Many of them may not post their rates but deal on a one-on-one basis.

Before you pick a device, consider the following considerations.

- Marketing Automation BEST PRACTICES
- Outreach on Social Media
- Predicting Leads
- Individualized Material
- Emails that are conduct-based
- The growth of chatbots will continue
- Virtual and Augmented Reality

Are you either using or intending to buy digital tools? Follow those best practices and patterns. They're going to help you channel your energies to get the best results in the right way.

Outreach with Social Media

Around 58 percent of consumers on social media hold an update on social media brands. So, every day, organizations need to deal with a large client base.

In order to simplify these connections, automation tools like SocialDrift support. To interact with users by likes, tweets, and follows, it utilizes a machine-learning algorithm.

Predict Leads

Lead scoring is created by automation. By automated lead scoring, marketers may classify top performing platforms. One such forum is Infer. To determine which prospects are likely to turn into customers, it uses probability calculations.

Personalized Content

Why are Netflix and Amazon and other platforms so tremendously successful? It has been shown that their personalized content is what attracts users. In the right way, it will engage listeners. Automation software using AI can boost marketers' abilities to produce personalized content.

Behavior-based emails

When a contact joins a particular workflow, services like Ad Espresso or LeadsBridge cause email advertising, so consequently, depending on his role in the funnel, a related message is sent to the prospect.

Chatbots will keep on growing.

According to the report, 70 percent of respondents choose to access a brand through a chatbot rather than an app, and 60 percent of users receive a request from a chatbot to respond to it. Chatbots will become more advanced and will be able to offer guidance and behavioral reactions.

The chatbot movement will continue to increase; consumer engagement will become more seamless.

Recipe #1 Chatbot with character

Ingredients: Chatbot software for your website or a social network (as Chatfuel, Drift, Landbot, aiaibot, HubSpot, Intercom, Birdeye and so on)

Method: First of all you collect a lot of possible questions and thoughts of your interests, prospects and leads. And you collect your answers to these questions. Then you define the kind of humor you will show in the answers and some language characteristics. In short: the character of your bot. Are there any jokes you do on a regular basis while talking to your future customers? Attach them to the bot.

Now comes the tricky part. Assemble all of the above to some well-orchestrated dialogues.

Difficulty: Intermediate

Purpose: With chatbots, you can foster your customers' experiences and you can qualify your leads automatically, if you build in some important lead qualification questions you would otherwise ask the lead on the phone.

Total time: Calculate with some two days of work before your bot 1.0 is setup and running.

Virtual and Augmented Reality

In the area of robotics, VR will open up new possibilities. Companies would be able to supply clients with ubiquitously enhanced experiences. AR will make marketers more engaging, as well. By 2022, sales of AR goods are anticipated to hit about $117.4 billion. For advertisers, this would create an integrated environment; they will provide consumers with a real-life product and service experience. As a result, more prospects could be involved, a higher number of leads produced, and more conversions could be generated.

Current Top Marketing Automation Software

The entire marketing tool ecosystem in 2020 is wide and confounding. There are several redundant services; for them, many overlapping instruments are planned.

We will look at a list of top SMB marketing automation tools.

EngageBay: one of the best end-to-end marketing, sales & service automation applications, which covers significant facets of lead segmentation, email models for automation, personalization of communications, and several other resources.

Outfunnel: an analytics platform for revenue marketing and deep integration and CRMs to keep both sales and marketing synchronized.

HubSpot: It is an inbound marketing program that allows lead generation via email marketing, and provides the sales department with additional support attachments.

Pardot: It is a B2B program developed to enhance the marketing and sales teams' productivity. Due to pricing, this is a solution rather for larger companies.

Marketo: This software is highly focused on consumer experience.

MailChimp: It offers tools through a strong email marketing campaign to maximize automation, and is used by thousands of startups as its usage is really fun. (However, it does not mean that the other solutions mentioned here are not).

Key-Takeaways

The main criteria for a well-planned and smooth approach for automation are:

A goal-oriented marketing methodology can produce leads and transform them into clients.

It offers productivity and aims to make work simpler for advertisers.

As per current business trends, marketing automation will continue to expand. Direct to the masses your marketing plan, but keep it personal.

This will save time, improve productivity, and maintain a smooth workflow. To best support the market, it can teach you potential data processing skills.

An automation approach focuses on company priorities, as well. It is very important to select the resources that better serve your organization and reap advantages over time.

As Jonathan Mildenhall said, "Going forward, selling in real-time will be the holy selling grail." Over time, you have to adjust and respond to the changing trends of the industry.

To help small companies decide: few important FAQs:

1. *Do I need marketing automation as a small business owner?*

To get founded and walk down the road of progress, small companies go through many struggles. Various activities may be streamlined to reduce the workload and promote market development due to insufficient funds and human capital. Some believe that such a broad company can incorporate marketing automation and profit from it. However, it isn't the case here. Only to determine your needs and evaluate what you will appeal to organizations of all sizes.

2. *How is this automation going to help me grow exponentially?*

Marketing automation for both B2B and B2C has many advantages, regardless of the size of an enterprise. We would like to clarify certain points since we have already addressed the benefits of using automation in depth.

It saves time by streamlining long processes such as campaign building, agreeing on the right timetable, comparing outcomes of split studies, etc.

Better lead parenting through the use of current consumer data and study of lead trends.

Great consumer service by delivering a tailored experience with them. In consumer loyalty, revenue, and customer engagement, personalized content often assists.

Helps the sales and marketing departments to maximize. This tends to free money for significant marketing, a new generation of leads, etc. This would also help you to flourish without attracting a new workforce.

To ensure greater communication and flow of relevant information, more stable and productive workflows.

3. *What are the basic characteristics that I can watch out for?*

Any of the basic characteristics to review are:
- User-friendly, simple interface

- Integration with CRM
- Good Landing Pages
- Social Media Management
- Lead Nurturing Capabilities
- A/B Testing
- Insightful analytics

4. *Is the program for automation too costly to set up and manage?*

According to your company's needs and, of course, your budget, you need to select an automation program. When you have a specified target, your wallet would not be heavy from the right service provider. So, analysis, appraisal, and purchasing are relevant.

EngageBay, known for its optimum solutions at competitive prices, is - in my eyes - one of the best in the industry. Their full-featured implementation takes care of all the specifications, especially if you look for small business automation. They can take care of everything, from personalization to segmentation, to lead nurturing. They could be the ultimate all-in-one solution that your company needs with its efficient sales & support automation features!

5. *Could both the distribution and marketing teams use it?*

For both sales and marketing, marketing automation may assist and improve ROI. In addition, the gathered knowledge can be used for improved lead generation and lead nurturing by both teams. This can be used to concentrate on the effective advertisement and advertising as well.

Lead Scoring And Lead Nurturing

What is the main task your salespeople do for success? Most sales reps confirm "nurturing leads" is the one key activities for growth.

As shown in the graph above, lead nurturing is one activity that organizations use the most in marketing automation. The capability of nurturing leads is one of the greatest advantages of marketing automation. This ensures that partnerships can be built with prospective buyers who are not yet willing to buy, but maybe more nurturing. Marketo notes that nurturing "could lead to 50% more revenue leading to a 33 % lower cost per lead." Lead nurturing is triggered by emails sent to clients to persuade them to buy. This approach helps them get to a "sale-ready" state.

Behavioral analysis systems that display businesses and the individual web pages accessed by customers are especially helpful. It will also demonstrate the kinds of content that prospects are interested in, allowing companies to realize which methods to take when marketing and closing the sale to consumers. Messages can be submitted to prospects to pique their attention based on the information they have studied. Since clients perceive this data to be extremely important to them, they are more likely to buy it.

This knowledge will be fed to the sales staff, helping sales have smoother, more knowledgeable interactions with prospective clients, understanding whether clients have taken action on the company's website, and specifically, the action is taken.

Lead scoring is also incredibly useful to help organizations realize which leads they can work on. The automated lead scoring method helps to screen leads to their involvement in the business.

This tends to distinguish real prospective clients of concern from others who, for example, may have been doing testing and who are not interested in purchasing. Those with a higher score will be targeted for the most eligible leads, and this emphasis avoids promotion and promotional effort that would otherwise be wasted on impossible targets.

Increasing Revenue

The improvement in revenue that is available when these technologies are introduced in an enterprise is one of the most important overall advantages of marketing automation and, at the same time, one of the best reasons why marketing automation makes sense. For a number of common purposes, this is done with marketing automation technologies. The willingness to work with leads and ultimately continue to generate greater market conversions is highly significant, and contributes to improved corporate revenues. It is also possible to see what has succeeded in nurturing leads by achieving greater lead conversion through a marketing automation method, and focusing on these methods in the future, saving the company time and resources. This suggests that success improves as well.

Around the same time, marketing automation technologies allow retailers to further concentrate on cross-selling and up-selling operations to bring more sales from current buyers. Making all consumer information available from the same system, which is often connected to the enterprise's CRM system, is accomplished by further identifying individual customer needs. Growing sales will ultimately have an added benefit of growing sustainability, which is a big factor as to why the introduction of marketing automation programs makes sense for most organizations.

Consolidation of Multiple Systems

Marketing automation has proved particularly useful for consolidating different marketing systems or repositories of customer data and bringing them all together into one system. For example, many organizations have different web analytics systems, marketing via email, dealing with landing page marketing, and social media marketing. Marketing automation helps enterprises eliminate these varied processes, and aims to work on marketing operations within one system.

Because all information about prospective customers is stored in one method, this means that CRM activities are much smoother to execute, since the customer contact can be done from the stage that they enter the system as a lead up to the period that they purchase from the company and through any after-sales procedures that take place. Marketing automation tools can be mixed in many ways with CRM applications to deal with this. This can also be achieved where enterprises have built their CRM systems in-house. All of this is vital because it allows firms to relate the different customer duties they undertake to ensure that everyone performs on the same overarching interests, and that what one team does is not in conflict with what another team does.

Edge Playing

Most companies have already adopted marketing automation systems. If competitors are not using marketing analytics tools, now is a smart time to get ahead. If these facilities are still used, then the business is playing catch up.

This is true for all B2B and B2C companies. One survey finds that 75% of US B2B businesses have been using marketing automation for more than one year now. Studies have shown that many businesses now explicitly purchase marketing analytics software to keep up with their rivals.

Nonetheless, many businesses also do not profit from the possibilities that marketing technology offers. A Salesforce study found that:

- 68% of firms have not identified or sought to quantify their revenue funnel.
- There is no proven lead nurturing process or toolset for 65 percent of enterprises.
- • 78% of marketing leads are not turned into sales
- There is a marketing lead certification framework for just 56 percent of companies.

These statistics indicate that by introducing a marketing automation system, there is already plenty of potential for companies to achieve a competitive advantage. If, however, the use of marketing automation technologies proceeds in the manner Gartner has expected, then the window will pass quickly to achieve this strategic edge. Companies should leap on this opportunity as soon as possible if they wish to stay ahead of their competitors.

Improve Customer Relationships with Customer Obsession

Marketing automation can better understand customers, which can improve an organization's relationships with these customers. By understanding what customers want and their main areas of focus and interest, conversations with customers can be optimized to emphasize those customers' areas of interest. This means clients are more likely to feel as if the organization hears their desires. The organization will better identify the consumer's needs, because it will have more knowledge stored on customer desires from the sales funnel to the point that a prospect has become a customer, and beyond. Smart companies may also connect this to customer support, as the customer experience can be preserved later from a history of knowledge on what consumers are asking for from a firm, based on knowing the customer's activities in the run-up to the transaction. If a client clicks on a white paper related to a particular topic, it is possible to store this knowledge about the client. This same knowledge and perception of the consumer will be later used by customer service agents to deliver improved service. This has the net effect of strengthening the relationship between the consumer and the firm.

In both sales and marketing, there is always friction. One side faults the other for not following up on the offered leads. The other says it was not good for the leads that were given. In certain companies, this is a never-ending source of irritation. Marketing automation tools help boost this situation because, among other activities, the device may provide reviews for prospects depending on how they communicate with the company's website.

To concentrate on topics of concern to those consumers, conversations with consumers should be tailored.

This provides sales information, which helps salespeople know where they should invest time to sell to customers. It also shows salespeople clearly which of the leads are not worth wasting time on, such as students researching academic papers and other website users who are not necessarily interested in purchasing an organization's products or services. Poor leads never need even to be passed on to sales at all, and instead, sales can focus on the leads that are likely to turn into customers.

Marketing automation tools provide greater visibility regarding both sales and marketing teams' activities and performance, which shows managers where things are working well and where improvements are needed. This, too, aims to improve sales and marketing teams' organizational productivity and efficacy. Consistency and coordination between the distribution and marketing departments' tasks can be accomplished, which allows them to coordinate, interact, and collaborate more between the two roles. With marketing automation programs in operation, the sharing of information, in particular, can be vastly enhanced. All this helps push up the return on investment obtained in the company by both sales and marketing functions.

Marketing automation ties the two departments together in terms of the specifics of the different marketing and sales teams' activities. Lead qualification can be automated from the marketing side, and the assignment of leads can be automated. Revenues can be best connected to individual campaigns, and clients can be sent tailored messages. From the sales viewpoint, through behavioral monitoring, it is possible to grasp prospect behavior, get real-time alerts on prospect activity, cultivate buyers, and find all the data needed in one location to close the deal. Combining all of these activities helps to create efficiencies in the sales process to both functions.

Marketing Automation Benefits for Small Businesses

It used to be a lot more daunting than it is now to take the entrepreneurship community's first steps. It is possible to launch our goods and services to the world across digital platforms and opportunities for new clients. For both B2B and B2C businesses, social media and digital marketing have been critical for an organization to achieve success. New ideas, such as inbound marketing, have arisen and impacted the way we engage with consumers.

Small companies have found themselves in a modern, fairer world, where they have all the requisite resources to start engaging with the major players in the industry. One of the must-have technologies that any entrepreneur can invest in is marketing automation.

First steps before scaling

Even if your company is already selling to consumers or building land to "open for business," before dipping your head into the field of digital marketing automation, it is important to pause, draw plans and schedule every single move.

Bear in mind that for small businesses willing to simplify their digital media processes, this sort of transformation takes work, but it pays off after a while. Since small companies have minimal investment capital (and no unimaginable spending), the best approach is to build the following list before starting:

- Know the market and what you offer
- Know who the ideal purchasers (personas) are
- Know where these customers can find the goods.

- Know how the business can deal with these openings.
- Create an ultimate solution to digital marketing.

It appears to be so many. Perhaps this is why corporations sometimes may overlook building a marketing campaign. It's not a mystical computer that starts operating with the click of a button, even recognizing that marketing automation will streamline processes. Let's look at each step in a deeper way.

Define your market

Identify what you're offering, the competitive edge, and how rivals and the business surrounding you operate.

The first step to creating an assertive digital marketing campaign is to decide just what you can sell to your customers. Define who, how, when, and when your firm will contact prospective clients.

Know your personas

You've got to know more about the clients who would buy from you. What their jobs are, where they live; what challenges they're trying to solve; what solution they're looking for; what they hope from the solution; what kind of social media or forum they're surfing, what kind of pizza they love, and so on. The more details you have on them, the more targeted and accurate your activities can be in digital marketing.

What are your distribution channels?

It's here that you share the news for yourself. As it is still possible to automate inbound marketing, any digital marketing campaign must include a website and a blog. A great range of businesses can use social media. There are so many different platforms, organizations, and forums out there that address at least one topic that could be easily addressed by your product.

Again, that is why it comes first to know the business and the ideal purchasers. You'll only be able to select and improve behavior in the right ways with this knowledge.

Establish your communication channels

Where will you be when customers want you? More important: as they get involved in your bid, how can they hit you? In your website, forum, email, and on-site massages, a digital marketing campaign often involves contact pages. In-app alerts, push notifications, and VOIP solutions (through app integrations) can be used for SaaS and web companies.

Provide the right places to locate you for leads and opportunities. Always make sure that someone from your industry is there exactly when they need your answer to support your soon-to-be-customers. If you respond more quickly than your rivals and deliver customized marketing service, you can also win some points with them. Just guess what? For all these things, automation will support you.

Develop your digital marketing strategy

You are able to develop a digital marketing strategy for your small company, now that you have lots of knowledge about your industry, your ideal clients, and the way they can enter your company. Marketing automation requires a well-defined digital marketing plan, and all processes are strictly related; from lead generation to customer retention.

Your business will be able to optimize the operations with automation after you build your plan. It sounds like a boatload of work, but don't be scared. After implementation, things get way easier.

Marketing automation for small businesses

In general, small companies suggest strict budgets, limited headcount, and an everlasting lack of time. Exactly how marketing automation can help is there.

Automation technologies that go beyond lead nurturing and customer interaction will offer many advantages to your business. Any of them are here:

It saves consumer retention time and effort. Inbound marketing seamlessly suits digital procedures, unlike cold calls and other more orthodox modes of a consumer approach. This means a content management approach compatible with the marketing and sales pipeline, where nearly effortless consumers can be transferred automatically during it.

It decreases the errors that can happen between systems. Since all the marketing and sales funnels are "rolling" in the same location, leads and opportunities are related and can be easily reached on the same network. Technology like this will hold it in one place instead of searching through multiple instruments to locate a single piece of data.

It is simpler for personalization and hypersegmented texts. Most people believe that automation means a less human, more robotic approach to clients, but to create customized approaches, automated systems may use knowledge from leads and prospects. That, of course, whilst approaching them, without losing the "personal touch" required.

It strengthens the way firms treat leads and clients. Lead procurement, nurturing, and conversion optimization activities should be taken advantage of by both small and large companies, even though there is not a full team able to handle it. Lead scoring will help organizations decide who is prepared for a call and who needs a little more content to make their minds productive.

The main thing about automation is that most of the features enable organizations to concentrate on a keystream of income that is sometimes overlooked: existing clients. This reliable source of income is especially important for rising corporations. Marketing technology will help you guarantee that, as you expand your client base, life-long buyers and brand evangelists are healthy, continuously finding opportunities for upselling and cross-selling.

Bear in mind that the method should be periodically revisited, updated, and tailored for the best outcomes.

The most reliable resource for a small company looking to expand in 2017 is marketing automation. More than 49 percent of enterprises from all types of sectors now use marketing automation, and month after month, this adoption continues to expand. It emerges as organizations gradually learn that automating their systems improves efficiency from purchase to conversion and beyond.

Using the tips we gave you, do not forget to create a great digital marketing campaign and come to us again later to share the performance.

What is the robotics of marketing? You have most definitely come up with this issue if you have been an active user of email marketing tools.

Feeling like you get chills from the term?

No reason for fears. Let's break down the meaning of marketing automation in marketing today. Grab a coffee cup and learn: Marketing automation for small firms vs. big enterprises

- Marketing automation & data
- Campaign automation advantages
- Examples of marketing automation
- Project management for automation marketing

Marketing automation is a program that is designed to automate routine marketing activities (such as emails) and make more targeted and customized consumer contact.

You might be wondering:

Should my marketing team use marketing automation technologies?

The answer is yes.

A whopping 75 percent of marketers say they are already using marketing automation technology in the State of Marketing Automation Survey by socialmediatoday.com.

Is marketing automation ideal for small companies only?

Marketing automation is advantageous for your enterprise, regardless of your market size and sector. It's not a question of whether to use marketing automation these days, but rather a question of what to do.

By automating regular emails, some firms can enjoy the advantages of marketing automation, while others can benefit from its lead scoring functionality.

Usually, SMEs consist of persons sporting lots of hats. These firms can use marketing automation to get rid of manual labor and run tailored campaigns with fewer resources. To manage vast masses of fragmented consumer data, marketing automation is necessary for larger organizations.

Automation & Data for Marketing

Without using info, automation technology gives little benefit. Therefore, you need to incorporate the platform for marketing automation into a channel from which the data can be collected and used in specific marketing campaigns.

Your marketing platforms, depending on your business, can be:

- CRM
- Website

Forum for Email marketing

- Smartphone Mobile App
- Tool for case scheduling
- Social Media

Internet Shop or Machine ERP

You should begin gathering email subscribers if you are looking to use email as your automation channel. You would have a base for sending tailored messages in this manner. Here are lots of tips on how to build your list of addresses.

Project management for automation marketing

It is all about the individuals that are helping you meet your business goals. Be sure that the automation initiative includes a well-organized team.

You ought to have, at least, in order to handle marketing automation like a pro:

Someone from the communications department or also an in-house expert for marketing automation

To have input on the consistency of leads and transactions, as well as sales management.

External or in-house IT support for integration processing and other technological problems.

How to Find a Small Business Marketing Automation Software

It is, by no means, simple to pick a small business marketing automation program. There are so many decisions that will leave a marketer frustrated. You wind up worrying about—

Will it have all the campaign automation capabilities that my company needs?

Will I be able to use any of the marketing automation platform features?

I've got a CRM. Do I need a platform to automate marketing?

Small business owners and advertisers are working on a minimal budget to add to that.

So, not only do they have to satisfy the demands of promotions, but they also have to accommodate the department of accounting.

How will a tool for marketing automation be better than CRM software?

You may think it's an insane idea to plug in a CRM program sub-section while talking about marketing automation platforms. You can find it useful if you are a CRM loyalist.

CRM software's primary purpose is to control the sales pipeline. Other features are merely add-ons. If you look at a CRM architecture, it has a database, and by requests, most modules communicate with it.

To meet certain needs of the marketing department, modern CRM software has outgrown this concept. The CRM program is not designed at its heart to simplify, well, anything!

You can't do that with a CRM if you want to send emails that possess complex content. You can't do that with a CRM if you want to A / B search your emails.

Likewise, in most CRM software, email-based lead nurturing is not practical, but it remains a significant marketing function. Without due diligence in the first place, you can't just assume that all your leads will hand you their currency.

I may go on and on about the inadequacy of CRM technologies and the need for good marketing automation.

Bearing in mind these CRM program shortcomings (and before closing this page), let's move on to why you should care about automating the marketing.

Tips For Selecting The Best Marketing Automation System

An ever-expanding ocean is the realm of marketing automation. Companies also require a dedicated budget so as to pick the correct collection of marketing instruments.

Many organizations do not have the time, resources, or individuals to choose a tool for marketing automation. So, of course, they're looking for an all-in-one marketing platform.

Understanding a marketing automation tool's services empowers advertisers to create educated choices.

This piece is intended to show you how to pick applications for small business marketing automation. When you browse for marketing automation, we'll be asking about what capabilities you might expect. To help you compare small business marketing automation tools, we will also provide some ideas.

In the end, we will also bring you to some of the most comprehensive tools in the industry for marketing automation.

You should be aware of the marketing automation platform (MAP) capabilities.

To build a list of what marketing automation functionality you require, you could use these suggestions. Use it then to compare various software for small companies for marketing automation.

These capabilities come from insight and analysis into the world of marketing automation software.

Progressive Profiling

Who doesn't want free equipment, right? Yet, since it's a free resource, individuals do not want to waste any time purchasing it. Analysis has shown that reducing type lengths improves conversion rates.

No client needs to waste time completing the forms. For their shortened attention span, users of the site are legendary. If you ask them to fill out the 9-field form for a free e-book, these visitors will close the tab.

This idea is put to use by Radical profiling. It helps you create the client's profile over time by asking for fewer details than a full-fledged information type.

If users like it, they can come back to use the asset or use other properties from your platform. You can query them for more information in another short form when they do. This scheme has the potential over time to become a predictor of lead maturity too.

Tip: Verify whether a marketing automation program supports radical profiling. See how many details, and how many passes it captures. Does it have multi-stage, conditional opt-in forms with inbuilt capabilities?

TARGETED EMAIL CAMPAIGNS

Email personalization helps boost open rates and click rates. The buying pipeline provides a beneficial start, and the landing page will pick up from there.

In email personalization, the first move is to segment the email list based on common factors. This list of influences; geography, behavioral, socioeconomic, among others, can be whatever you choose.

This personalization tends to bring your clients closer to you. This will trigger open email rates and conversion rates to rise instantly.

Tip: Social logins accumulate massive volumes of user data (Facebook, Twitter, and Gmail). By testing how they use social data, you can check how clever a marketing automation platform is.

Integration of all three websites, CRM, and automation of marketing

Marketing automation integration with the website, and CRM completes the ecosystem of lead production. It helps robust consumer insights to be extracted. Complementary knowledge about leads is found in both systems.

We can harness the strength of marketing analytics when paired with website behavior monitoring.

Tip: Ask the marketing automation technology sales staff about how broad their website and CRM integration is. For what data it requires from the two, you can get answers as well as how it requires them.

Visitor Activity Tracking

Data obtained from social logins can be paired with data obtained from the website for visitor activity monitoring. You will segment your email list even more, until you realize just what the consumer is interested in.

This is one of the most effective ways of personalizing your emails; it's almost a guarantee of your emails' effective conversion rates.

Tip: Make sure the marketing automation tool informs you about any visitor's experience from the first page to the exit page. The more stats they have, the better it will be for your segmentation.

Sales teams need each client to have a pulse. Tracking websites and email activities will help observe the client's path; from a fresh lead to a paid client. Personalized email updates and cold calls can minimize the duration of this trip.

The sales staff send up automatic sales reminders to tip them off to clients close to making a buying decision. Some applications for marketing automation often immediately allocate the sales reps to eligible leads.

The requirements for certification must be 'customizable by the organization' and not the instrument itself.

There should also be a customer information panel right next to it for real-time updates. A simple reference after the assignment gives ample details to the salesperson. It boosts the probability of easily closing the deal.

Tip: Personalized sales notifications should be allowed on a successful marketing automation platform. It encourages the sales staff to use their experience and not completely rely on the sales-boosting tool.

Lead Scoring and Lead Grading

The lead score shows how far in the sales funnel the customer has gone. The lead grade is for the fit of your product with the profile of the consumer. Both are complementary and not interchangeable ratings.

The concept is to consider the purpose and adaptation of the product consumer. This is one of the most popular aspects of marketing automation. For the conversion rate of all sales methods, a higher, more detailed lead consistency is higher: cold calls, emails, landing pages, etc.

Tip: The rule of law here is customization. Be sure that the platform for marketing automation allows for personalized lead scores and ratings.

Nurturing Lead

Nobody will open their wallets and give you their money. The productivity of sales reps is severely impacted if the lead contact cannot make a buy.

In a traditional distribution channel, lead capture accompanies a convincing email strategy.

This is referred to as the multi-touch email program with a set of emails sent to the leader's email. The aim is to inform and reassure the buyer about the item. He connects with the marketing ecosystem when the customer opens the email. As he pushes further down the sales funnel, closer to a purchase, his lead score grows.

Based on the lead ranking, you can personalize your addresses. This "drip email campaign" approach helps save time; sales reps can only work on leads that are extremely likely to convert.

Tip: Most drip email strategy models should provide an effective marketing automation tool.

Forms and Landing Pages

No one needs to fiddle with passwords, so they don't have a mistake that tears down their landing page. The criteria in a marketing automation tool for a landing page feature are:

Multiple customizable templates for landing pages that can be deployed within minutes

Customized material for the landing page for each guest

Unlimited A / B checks, analytics, and the ability for optimization-one landing page architecture are never enough!

Customizable readymade models help remove all these issues. For such landing pages, they can also significantly minimize time-to-live.

Tip: Your framework for marketing automation should help you configure the content of the landing page. This customization should be dependent on the purchasing point, location, and other attributes of the lead. Some of the better ones also allow you to configure the content of your CTA and opt-in type. All this translates into improved rates of conversion.

Dynamic Content

The King is the client. Why not give what he needs to the king?

How do you know what the King wants? The question is: There are very specialized approaches to help you execute consumer personalization in marketing automation.

For a lead score/grade, location, source, geographic location, or any other attribute, you must pick the values. After that, you pick the interactive material you want to reveal for a group of leads meeting the set parameters. You can also pick these classes' place to view dynamic information, such as blogs, forms, landing pages, or emails.

Dynamic content thus helps you set a customer-specific version of your website's content on multiple digital properties.

For the tourist, higher personalization means greater reliability. This is a powerful opportunity for automation tools for small business marketing to improve conversion.

Tip: Search for a site that brings personalization beyond the lead score's characteristics and common text. A clever way of personalizing is to mine data and deep analytics through website behavior monitoring. It helps discover powerful resources for optimization.

Closed-Loop Reporting

Marketing isn't a blind investment anymore these days. I say that advertisers can't only get cash for "branding and recognition" through "blind spending."

Today, messaging goes way further than just two terms. Strong return-on-investment (RoI) must be able to back up the investments.

How does the automation of ads help you measure RoI?

Marketing works out promotions and gathers a set of leads. In the database, these leads are registered and forwarded to the sales team to follow up. The sales team will rely on the actions of the marketing team to get the leads in.

All sorts of marketing-generated leads go to sales without any recognition. Sales are usually not conscious of how the lead in the first place was obtained.

A tiny business marketing program associates each lead with the closed campaign by closed-loop reporting. With this, the marketing staff gets to know which platforms and campaigns have performed best. Daily review of this knowledge by marketing analytics may also offer insights into the success of campaigns.

Marketing automation thus allows the estimation of your marketing strategies' absolute return on investment.

There's also a secondary profit. The marketing staff's lead capture activities are still counted; revenues don't erase all the credits for closing the lead.

Tip: Ask for a comprehensive description of the sales staff about this before choosing a marketing automation tool. Tell them precisely what kind of insights will be accessible about campaign results.

Currently in the market, surveying marketing automation tools.

There are many major features for marketing automation software capabilities, but if you are prepared to pay the bill, there are a few "luxury" features available.

There are many marketing and CRM resources on the market, and every month, more are introduced.

What characteristics are acceptable for growing your own company? Inside your budget, which method gives you these characteristics?

It is impossible to locate one method that fits the company's specific market needs and budget allocation.

You have to be mindful of marketing automation to judge them on merit, but you still have to step beyond the shiny marketing copy to get facts about those tools.

Here are the most common ways of launching research in the field of marketing automation.

1. EngageBay

At EngageBay, we have understood the requirements of small companies and their budgetary limitations. We also developed a low price tool that combines marketing, distribution, and service automation functions.

The Sales-optimized CRM of EngageBay enables you to split your sales pipeline into phases, allowing you to build a sales board with various sales pipelines in the Kanban format. Deals will be delegated to different team members on each pipeline, and there will be appropriation of activities that they need to perform on their deals.

To nurture your brand relationships using customized emails, you can equally rate the leads and create email sequences.

It also offers a full suite of workflows for marketing automation software, and A / B (Split) checks to optimize them. Also included in this module are email performance and customer behavior review.

With EngageBay, to appear more open and welcoming to your clients, your customer support team does not have to sacrifice internal productivity. To ensure your customer stays at the forefront of attention for your Customer Support team, our Support Bay has implemented the Flywheel principle.

Canned answers and group service passes may be submitted to them. For smaller teams facing high ticket sizes, the process management capabilities can further hasten the service time. Finally, they will concentrate on the most relevant clients and only on tickets with a high effect.

What sets EngageBay apart from other marketing automation suppliers is our email and landing page template customization kits.

While most email and landing page programmers allow design elements to be drag-and-drop, each new segment's actual design takes a long time to prepare and authorize within the team. Our designers further raised the norms.

With EngageBay, creating personalized parts for your emails and landing pages will not waste valuable hours (or even minutes) of your day. From one of the built-in segment models, you can pick and press to insert one at the chosen spot.

And even the section models, as you can see, are categorized into divisions, depending on the types of section content.

We have personalized pricing options that start from a little over $7 per user/month to just over $47 per user/month for our all-in-one approach. EngageBay's pricing delivers the best bang for every penny of your marketing budget if you're a solopreneur looking for a stable, all-in-one distribution, support, and marketing network.

Head over to our Pricing page to find the most acceptable package and tailor the package according to your particular needs.

2. ActiveCampaign

With subscription formats, list segmentation, conditional email content, and split checking, it helps you move beyond email marketing. Using email marketing, you can nurture long-term company partnerships with your executives.

Also, it makes you:

Design the funnel for automation

Understand how clients are navigating into the funnel

Relieve any bottlenecks in their buying journey to drive them down the funnel quicker.

You may also attribute the source of leads on each record, apart from tracking leads. To help you allocate deals to your participants so as to help them close these deals more efficiently, their CRM is streamlined.

Overall, with responsive support staff, ActiveCampaign is accessible, intuitive, and creative.

3. HubSpot

Because of its consistent branding and content management efforts, HubSpot has retained its strong industry position. If you're a small enterprise, HubSpot would be loved by you. Its analytics are very strong, and it is intuitive and simple to understand the overall UI.

This is why it's shocking that they have an on-boarding and preparation fee of $500-$3000 (depending on the package you purchase). HubSpot is costly to get started, and it gradually becomes ever more costly as the email list expands.

Their free plan includes an email list only for restricted use with few marketing automation features.

You will have to spend $12,600 to get started with the professional package (having some good marketing automation features).

4. GetResponse

Concerning Email Marketing, GetResponse offers email templates and autoresponders for campaign setup. Also, it ensures:

Optimized email arrival times for any customer

Customization of the time zone and send hours

A dedicated department for ensuring high deliverability of emails.

Scalable process models, dynamic segmentation filters, and automatic workflows for retargeting contacts who leave their carts are part of the GetResponse marketing automation kit. Any activity on the website made by a lead or a client is monitored, and it impacts the lead ranking.

They also have code-free and mobile-optimized landing pages, with a promise that in less than 30 minutes, you can create deployment-ready landing pages.

You can also set up flexibly-timed webinar registrations with GetResponse, and give your attendees email reminders. With their webinar program, outside of GetResponse, consumers won't have to interface with extra apps.

Expect to spend anywhere from $14 / month to a little over $1,500 / month, following a 30-day free trial with GetResponse.

For the first 1,000 contacts, their simple package offers all of their email marketing characteristics. If you like webinars, landing pages, CRM, or marketing automation, you need an update.

5. Ontraport

Using Ontraport, with landing pages and lead catch forms, you can expand your email list. You will also have good features for email marketing and SMS marketing.

With detailed and reliable results, Ontraport users will have access to its marketing analytics and immersive monitoring features. For any of the pipeline leads, you will use these experiences to enrich the marketing experience.

Ontraport includes a drag-and-drop designer, and a wide library of pre-built models for landing pages, icons, buttons, and forms for effective landing page creation. The pages of Ontraport can also be modified with interactive content.

As opposed to other marketing automation tools, Ontraport's pricing policies are pricey. Their simple package begins at $79 per account per month, and has 1,000 contacts as the upper cap. Additional users come in at $47 a month/user. There are no stages in terms of functionality, i.e. both plans have all of their functionality. Based on their service packages, their price policies are distinguished.

Their most costly package (Enterprise package) provides for $497 a month for five account holders.

Small companies often make the wrong decisions when choosing marketing automation applications, but they do not need to. The marketing automation platform provides many top-of-the-line features for small companies. This provides a deeper view of the consumers' profiles. This makes for greater personalization and higher rates of conversion. We may then extend this personalization to multiple channels of communication.

6 Marketing Automation Mistakes You Must Avoid

Marketing automation is increasingly rising, and its benefits are being taken advantage of by many businesses. 51 percent of businesses are using marketing automation, according to research by Emailmonday, and more than half (58 percent) expect to implement it.

But while marketing automation is achieving mass acceptance, the bad news is that people can make many automation errors. These errors can range from email spamming, to not incorporating automation within the database of the organization. And worse, some of these common mistakes could end up ruining a campaign and/or harming the reputation of a brand.

Here are six errors to avoid when using marketing automation.

1. Beginning without a strategy

If you don't have a plan in place, marketing automation would likely fail.

A survey by Three Deep Marketing found that because of the lack of an effective strategy, 58 percent of marketers thought they were having difficulty achieving success with automation tools and, of course, it is difficult to produce results without a plan to direct automation efforts.

It is essential to define campaign priorities and targets before getting started with automation. The aim of the campaign, for instance, could be to generate leads or increase open rates for emails, each objective requiring a different strategy.

It is necessary to take the time to create a marketing automation strategic plan that involves defining targets, segmentation, integrations, content, and other components.

2. Irrelevant material Blasting

It's simple to build and schedule campaigns quickly with marketing automation software - but it's also easy to go overboard and blast too many emails or social media posts that aren't essential to your audiences.

Spamming the inboxes of your contacts can result in higher unsubscription rates in terms of email, which not only costs you contacts, but can also lead to account suspension from email service providers.

Make sure the audiences are segmented, and just submit appropriate emails at the right time to the right people. To avoid bombarding your contacts, you should also look to better stagger them.

For example, to personalize content based on where consumers are in the purchaser's journey, a real estate agent might segment their email list. While homeowners may be interested in repairs, property taxes, or insurance material for the first time, buyers looking to sell their homes are interested in topics such as tips for house staging or how to price a home. Note, the content must always add value to the reader, so submit only useful and essential material.

Social media may annoy followers to share so much content that is not centralized on a particular subject or industry. Individuals are using social media to be social, which underlines the need to have useful and engaging content.

To be effective, marketing automation solutions have to integrate the other tools and databases of an organization. Otherwise, to develop customized customer interactions, automation tools would not connect with other systems or utilize user data.

89 percent of users who have implemented marketing automation systems have combined them with their CRM systems, according to ResearchCorp. A holistic approach to data management is enabled by such integration and can significantly increase customer experiences.

And although many marketing automation tools can communicate with other instruments and systems, organizations can also use applications for data management to help them combine solutions for automation.

3. To set it and to forget it

Falling into the "set it and forget it" mode is one of the biggest risks of using marketing automation.

Adopting this form of strategy will not allow you achieve optimum results. While marketing automation saves time by automating manual tasks, someone still needs to take care of campaigns and track them.

Users can check in on automated campaigns regularly and monitor their performance to catch any mistakes or unexpected effects.

A trigger could not function properly, for example, or as a result of the automation phase, there may be a lack of interaction. Monitoring each campaign helps organizations stay updated on what's going on and, if necessary, stop the campaign and make adjustments. Otherwise, a campaign that is not successful would keep on being unsuccessful.

4. No testing or optimization

Content testing is a vital component of marketing automation, helping companies learn more about their audience and determine whether a strategy or campaign will succeed or not. Then, to refine campaigns based on effects, users may make adjustments.

For instance, users may perform A / B testing to optimize their email marketing automation tool's capabilities. They can create two versions and compare components, such as the subject line, CTA, or sender address, instead of producing only one version of a campaign. To find out why something is working, be sure to only evaluate one variable at a time.

For instance, real estate agents can test their email subject lines by sending their email to a smaller section of their list to see which one convinces customers to open, and then automatically send the winning subject line to the rest of their audience. They might find that a question like" Are you still looking in the X neighborhood? "works better than a statement like" Check out these X neighborhood properties.

Testing how emails appear on various devices and designing them responsively is also relevant.

Social media can also be checked; checking your social media post CTAs is crucial. Maybe it just doesn't work to "learn more," but there's something else that gets people to click the post. Be sure to try how well different hashtags work by writing longer and shorter posts (on the networks that allow).

5. Reliance on the wrong metrics

It's easy to get excited by a high-performing metric and neglect other essential numbers while evaluating an automated campaign's success. Don't get distracted - to get the full picture and appreciate the effects of your efforts; make sure you dig deeper.

A high email open rate, for example, is nice to see, but this metric does not inherently mean that a campaign performs well. To measure a campaign's progress, look deeper at the click-through rate. Just because users open an email, it doesn't mean they're taking action.

When assessing an automated campaign's success, be sure to look at different metrics.

To prevent these errors, businesses that automate manual marketing activities should be vigilant. Marketing automation will certainly assist businesses to expand and increase their ROI when done correctly. Still, it can be easy to fall into simple traps and lulls that will derail the overall effort, as noted.

Part II: This is Sales Automation

Automate Leadgeneration And Boost Sales Numbers

"Complaining is silly. Either act or forget."

– **Joker**, Batman

In an ideal world, all sales staff will spend their days smoothly talking about an endless stream of ideal opportunities, close left and right high figure offers, and never break a sweat. But we do not live in a perfect world, and the hard work of prospecting is all about real sales.

Sadly, scouting is not glamorous. It's time-consuming, monotonous work that can bog down sales reps. Just 15% of the average salesperson's time is spent selling. The remainder of their day is spent on tedious tasks of the administrative type.

Prospecting is essential, but it is a dark hole of desperation that many sellers believe it does not have to be. We'll outline a proven system in this book to automate sales prospecting and boost sales numbers.

Intrigued? Let's get started then!

Advantages of automatic prospecting

Let's explore these first, before we hop into how to automate your sales prospecting efforts. Sales automation software has many advantages. It will help minimize your sales representatives' busy work, increase their morale, and increase the company's overall revenue.

Let's look at each of these benefits more closely:

1. Limit Busy Work

The first, most noticeable advantage of sales automation software is that the work sales reps need to do every day is significantly reduced.

With far less effort, activities such as scouring the internet for opportunities, mining LinkedIn for email addresses, and sending hundreds of customized emails can be done, which implies that sales teams have more time to sell and become more successful.

2. Sales Rep Motivation Boost

They will naturally be more inspired when sales reps are free to concentrate on what they do best and are not bogged down by boring administrative-type duties. Motivated team members work harder with more efficiency, and all great things help to raise workplace morale!

Sales automation systems eliminate most of the unattractive features of sales workers. So why wouldn't they be more inspiring to a sales rep that makes use of them?

3. Increase company sales

Higher company revenue would result from a highly motivated, super-productive sales team. It is almost unavoidable. Naturally, corporate income can rise if the team will spend more time selling and is motivated to perform at peak levels.

Sales automation software is, as you can see, extremely advantageous. But how do you make your distribution processes automated? In the next section, that's what we'll discuss.

Recipe #2: Autolike prospects posts on LinkedIn or Instagram

Ingredients: A tool like Phantombuster.

Method: In this tool, you set up a list of contacts from which you want to get noticed. And then you just say "autolike", and automatically you like every post of these contacts on LinkedIn or Instagram.

Difficulty: Beginner

Purpose: To build relationships smoothly.

Total time: 60 Minutes.

Attention: This automation might lead you to like some content you would not like personally. Some examples are likes on funeral images, or on posts with political opinions you don't share.

Outbound vs Inbound. Guiding principle of lead management

The difference between outbound and inbound sales and marketing is quite easy. In outbound, you reach out to a potential prospect via cold methods (mostly phone, email or texting) but in inbound, you will rather wait till the prospect reaches out to you. It is normally done via offering lead baits (could be pdf, audio, video and so on) on a landing page while asking for the email address in return. By the way, this is the core idea of lead management. This seems by far the better method. You don't have to do annoying phone calls, and you are in contact with really interested potentials. *So, which one is better?*

In my eyes this question does not make sense. Of course it is better to talk to someone interested in your products and services. BUT this only works if there is search traffic and interest in your offerings. If you are operating in a highly innovative field, there will not be much search volume, or if you are offering services nobody is searching for – for instance, let´s say some consulting services on "Use humor in your teams to have healthier work places").

If the latter is the case, you have to rely on cold calling artists and outbound prospecting. And that is the reason why this book covers both sides of the medal. Outbound and inbound. Both of them are highly automatable.

AUTOMATED PROSPECTING METHOD IN A PROVEN 4 STAGE

"We are about to let you in on a "secret formula" used by several top sellers if you've ever wondered," How do I automate sales? You will be able to spend far more of your time selling and less time doing boring, soul-sucking, administrative-type tasks once you've learned and implemented this automated prospecting method.

There are four phases to the system:

1. Choose the Best Tools for sales and prospecting automation

First of all, to help you reduce the time you spend on repetitive prospecting activities, you need to pick the correct sales automation tools.

In very simple terms, sales prospecting means looking for potential customers to grow the customer base of the business and generate revenue streams. Sales representatives spend most of their working hours on sales prospecting, day in and day out. Social media is used by the sales automation tool to create lead lists that include email, phone number, social profiles, and much more.

Sales reps have an ardent and time-consuming mission. Worse still, not all customers who show an intention will buy, either because they are not fully prepared to buy the product and are still waiting for the right time or are looking for cheaper alternatives. Some of these people may not even be genuine, or are suspects of cybercrime. You would like to be free of such elements in your prospect list and be a reliable information pool.

If you've ever worked in a sales team, you'd know that generating good quality leads takes a lot more time than reaching out to them. You will always struggle to find a system that saves you all that time and effort. That's where the image comes with sales prospecting tools equipped with sales automation. In a way, it makes the pace of sales more efficient and impactful.

Automation not only helps to find more leads in less time in outbound sales prospecting, but those leads found are of good quality, i.e. they have far better chances of becoming prospects. The sales team can relax with automation taking over. Sales automation software allows you to simply enter criteria as data entry points that you want your target prospects to meet, and the tool will give you a list of such target prospects along with all their verified information.

This book will address four sales prospecting automation tools that you can use to optimize your prospecting process to support sales teamwork easily.

Must Use tools for sales prospecting:

Anyleads

Anyleads is a software application that can be used by salespeople to automate prospecting for sales. Based on pre-selected parameters, it allows users to create reports with multiple data points. It also comes with an email seeker app that makes it easy to learn particular prospects' email addresses.

Speaking of email, it is simple to use the drag-and-drop editor included with Anyleads which has several eye-catching templates. It is also possible to plan and track pre-written messages to know exactly how well your promotions are doing.

As their tagline implies, Anyleads is far more than a software for sales prospecting automation. This sales automation tool also offers capabilities such as content generation and social media lead generation. The good thing is that this platform can be used by your sales team, whether you are a small business or a big company.

As of now, over 10000 companies use Anyleads as their sales prospecting automation tool. The ease of use it provides is what makes Anyleads distinctive from other sales automation tools. It is also one of the most sought after tools for sales automation because it has a great tracking ability that enables the sales team to engage effectively with their customers.

Let's look at some of the features under the umbrella of 'sales prospecting' offered by this sales prospecting software. We're not going to look at capabilities like content creation and lead generation, because they are beyond this article's scope. However, on Anylead 's website, you can read more about such functionalities.

Domain Enrichment, Emailing, Analyzing, Syncing, and Managing are the major features covered by Anyleads for automated outbound sales prospecting. Sub-functionalities for each of these functions exist. Let's dive deeper into this prospecting tool for sales:

Functionalities associated with the domain

Mining essential data entry and information from a pre-fed domain list is the first 'essential' job that this sales automation tool does for you. You simply need to upload domain names (in a list format). Sales prospecting automation tool – Anyleads - will generate all the company-related information for the sales team and more than 40 data points about all the employees working at this company.

Next, you can find a valid email address using a person's first name, last name, and company name. No need for email-hunter tools! You also choose to upload a list of company names, and the sales prospecting function of Anyleads will generate a domain name file related to those company names.

In a matter of minutes, you can check emails and get a list of only those email addresses that are valid.

Features/capabilities linked to the email

Begin by creating simple or complicated campaigns using the drag-and-drop editor of Anyleads.

Creating and editing your email templates. Their template editor for sales prospecting is neat and can be used by anyone!

Send your email with just a click to any site you want, or even to multiple senders.

Monitor and evaluate the success of your email campaign as soon as the hit button is sent. Track open rates, click rates, and one-dashboard conversions.

Export the statistics of your campaign results and preserve your documentation in Excel.

Capabilities Analyzing

Using this sales prospecting instrument, you can easily install the tracker code on your website. Once you have done that, you will start fetching some conversion stats from the campaigns you are running. The good thing is that you can use Anyleads to set up rules and do event tracking. So, at each stage of the funnel, you get to know how you are performing.

In an easily comprehensible and interpretable format, campaign insights are presented. You don't have to wrap your head around numbers, as in this sales prospecting software, there are visuals to explain everything.

Capabilities for synching and management

The first and very significant ability in a sales prospecting automation tool under 'synching' is sentiment analysis. With this feature in your toolkit, your email campaign's responses can be detected and sorted as 'positive' or 'negative' feelings/responses under the relevant columns in your list. For better categorization, you can create 'rules' and 'customize' for your sentiment analysis.

Based on the sense of responsibility, the sales team can move conversations to specific / predesignated folders. Sales automation eliminates the manual effort to sort and save responses in the corresponding folders.

The platform enables you to better import and export contacts, manage lists, and contact targets.

In addition to these sales prospecting features, as we have discussed before, it also provides content creation and B2B exchange features. Their pricing incorporates all functionality into a single package that enables all the suite functionality to be accessed and used unlimitedly. But yeah, they're a little pricey.

Their unlimited monthly package is slated at $489 / month. However, here's great news. They have a time-bound deal that enables you pay $99 / month forever. So, if you sign up now, you can make use of this awesome discount bid! They give a free trial for those who are not persuaded yet, so you can try it before buying it.

Update: Sales prospecting of Anyleads is all configured to comply with GDPR and CCPA requirements. Their legal teams analyze their practices and have introduced new features, such as the right to erasure, the right to rectification, the right of access, the right to entry and portability of data, and the right to restrict processing.

For modern sales teams seeking to automate their sales process, this Sales Prospecting Automation platform is a comprehensive platform. Prospect.io is bundled with all the good and smart features that an effective sales team must have in its arsenal, from email verification to drip campaigns to tracking campaign performance. It is an all-in-all lead generation tool that is better than most in the industry. And that is why it made it to our Top 4 list. Let's discuss some of the characteristics promised by Prospect.io.

Prospect.io assists with finding and verifying emails with utmost ease within 'sales prospecting.' In a matter of seconds or minutes, using Chrome extension on websites or social media profiles, you can find your prospect's information such as email ID, phone number, job title, etc. While searching for their email IDs and other details, you can either pick individual or bulk prospects on the list. You can also scan website domains with just as much ease and perform web page scan and individual search with Prospect.io. Your sales prospecting is sorted and streamlined with all of these capabilities in place!

In addition to these 'Sales Prospecting' specific features and functionalities, Prospect.io comes with emailing capabilities for sales automation, such as campaign tracking and synchronization. Together, all these features make Prospect.io one of the most sought-after online business lead generation and sales automation platforms. Because it is also essential to automate email and drip campaigns together with sales prospecting, there's a plus point to Prospect.io! It also simplifies your work further by helping you keep track of the success of email campaigns.

With their drip functionality, you can create email sequences automatically sent with this sales prospecting software. When a prospect responds or converts to the email, the campaign also automatically stops. It is also extremely simple to schedule emails with Prospect.io.

If you want to win in the optimization game, measuring your emails' performance is a key requirement. You will fill in the gaps and bottlenecks and improve your efforts only when you measure the click rates, impressions, and answers. If you are working on Prospect.io, you get complete reports that are easy to interpret.

Synching makes Prospect.io an increasingly competent tool to use for sales automation. Zapier, Slack, Salesforce, Pipedrive, Hubspot, and Close.io include some CRM integrations that add to Prospect.io's charm.

Would you like to know how Prospect.io is priced? Terrific! You are thinking in the correct direction. Let's see if the final deciding factor for you to buy or say bye to this sales prospecting tool is pricing.

On their pricing page, is the term 'credits' getting you all confused? Well, it did confuse me initially, too. But it's essentially pricing based on 'use.' Therefore, the more you use Prospect.io, the more benefit you get from the product, but it also means that the price gets higher. So, if you use Prospect.io's 1000 credits, you will pay around $99 / month for the object. If you like the item, you can try and start with this '1000 credit' plan and then pay extra for more use. That works for me!

Update on GDPR and CCPA:

Prospect.io has made clear to itself that they are ready for GDPR and CCPA. If you use Prospect.io as a sales prospecting tool, you can continue using it without any concerns related to GDPR and CCPA. Here are some of the highlights on their website that I came across:

- Updated conditions and service policies.
- An audit of all third parties to see if they are compliant with the GDPR and CCPA.
- Provided legal training for all employees to understand the complexities of GDPR and CCPA.

FindThatLead

Once again, I have listed an extremely easy-to-use sales automation tool. Hey, and why not? A good sales automation tool at the end of the day is easy for sales reps to work with. The two main capabilities offered by Findthatlead.com are 'verifier' and 'prospector.' These two terms are pretty self-explanatory. Still, just in case someone scrolled without reading about the other two items on my list and just landed on this one, here's a simple explanation:

Verifier: You can verify and validate an email identifier on your prospect list using an advanced algorithm in sales prospecting software.

Prospector: Look for the sales prospector's email address, website domains, telephone numbers, etc. using certain information you have, such as first and last name. Findthatlead has a specific and unique technique for prospecting, comprising three steps:

Segment: For your prospect hunt, pick specific segments. Segments could include business, industry, job title, place, etc.

Add info: Add specific details about the segments you have selected. For instance, if you have added the 'location' segment, type the location you want your prospects to be from.

Get Prospects: Findthatlead will provide a list of outcomes that you can use for sales prospecting based on the segments and their specific details.

The neat dashboard is the best part of using Findthatlead. You can manage several tasks from one dashboard, including lead management, domain search, lead search, prospecting, and CSV uploading.

Overall - I give Findthatlead 3.75 stars!

With the kind of pricing it offers, FindThatLead is an incredibly exciting sales prospecting tool. Concerning the pricing, guys, here's my take. Their basic plan begins at $0 / mo, and for the most costly one, rates are $1500 / month. Just like Prospect.io, you pay for usage or credits. So, for $1500 / month, the maximum credits you can use equals 18000. And, for $0, the minimum credit you can use is 50 / month.

Update: FindthatLead is compliant with the new laws of GDPR and CCPA protection, and all the latest updates on their website have been explained. For all customers who deal with data entry of EU citizens, GDPR and CCPA compliance is necessary.

Leadfuze

Leadfuze is a common application for the automation of prospecting for outbound sales. This helps users recognize opportunities based on their organizational positions, preferred sectors, the tech solutions they use, how much they spend on Adwords, and more. If you type in a few search parameters manually, the tool will help you locate the information you want.

You may use the app to find essential information such as email addresses, phone numbers, social media accounts, and other crucial information, until a few interesting leads are identified.

Another advantage of Leadfuze is that it integrates with many other common tools, such as HubSpot, Salesforce, G Suite, and Zapier. All in all, it's a pretty useful instrument for sales automation.

On Google, enter Leadfuze, and it takes you to a very refreshing website set in shades of orange. The layout is neat, and the product information is crisp. They introduce you to their sales assistant, a cherry on the cake - a bot that is completely prepared to assist you like your sales assistant. This virtual assistant, named Fuzebot, will build your list, verify emails, and make your entire process of prospecting more efficient.

Let's talk about all the features offered by Leadfuze to stack this sales prospecting tool up against the three other options I mentioned in this post.

Search: Make it simpler and faster to make tedious, manual search work. Specific target leads are based on criteria or segments, such as those with specific roles and industries, those using certain software, or those hiring, etc. Once that is done, based on your searched leads, you can unlock more data entry, such as their verified emails, phone numbers, social media profiles, and more!

Account-Based Selling: You can upload or input a domain or company name using Leadfuze. Then, select the roles that you want to target from their list. You will get a list of contacts close to your sales prospecting requirement, based on these criteria.

Bot Assistant: Right at the beginning, when presenting Leadfuze, I had already mentioned Fusebox. The bot is their special touch and makes it fun for customers to work with Leadfuze. But let's learn a little more about how this works:

Based on the criteria you have used as an input, the bot explores all over the web, as well as your data sources looking for leads. It adds them to your sales prospecting list once it finds relevant matches. The most significant task for which it is responsible is to ensure that the information it collects for you is accurate, verified, and updated. Fuzebot ensures that you can sit back and relax while it tracks and serves you leads on a plate.

1. It does all the hard work to validate and verify the emails on your list to ensure they are good to go.
2. It checks all of your current customers, subscribers, rivals, etc. that are already on your list. It sees that it does not repeatedly duplicate the reference to these contacts, so, it adds fresh new leads.

Leadfuze integrates seamlessly with well-known tools such as Close.io, Zapier, Pipedrive, Salesforce, Bidsketch, and more. A bit about integration.

What is absolutely, refreshingly awesome about Leadfuze is that they are on point and clear in their pricing. Starter, scaling, and custom is two plans for them.

1. Starter: For those who want to begin prospecting for their sales.
2. Scaling: For those who want their lead generation and recruitment efforts to scale up.
3. Custom: For those who in the other two plans need more lead credits than offered.

All of these plans are priced intelligently and are affordable enough not to make you feel like a hole in your pocket has been burned. Of course, if you have basic requirements, you can opt for their starter package, which is a fantastic choice based on the capabilities they offer.

Another thing to bear in mind is that while Leadfuze does not have a 'free trial,' it gives you 25 free lead credits to use. So, if you're not sure about opting for Leadfuze or any other sales prospecting tool, you can check out those 25 lead credits before signing up for their product.

GDPR and CCPA update: To ensure that their product is GDPR and CCPA compliant, LeadFuze has added new features. This includes the right to be forgotten, the right to access, the recognition of EU users to filter them out, the agreement on data processing, and many more.

To Wrap It Up

Based on functionality, I think that the best alternative is Leadfuze as far as sales prospecting goes. FindThatLead is the second-best on my list, and the reason being that it has a very easy to use dashboard. That kind of 'ease' is attractive. For me, Anyleads and Prospect.io fall into the same slot. I'll probably go for the one that suits my budget if I pick one of them.

Here is a one-on-one comparison that further lets me rate Leadfuze higher than any other alternatives. I used Prospect.io as well as Leadfuze. Both of these tools are extensions of Chrome that allow you to fetch web sales leads. Although Prospect.io integrates with profiles from Linkedin, it does not allow you to save prospects that you may want to target from this social media platform automatically. On the other hand, you can filter these prospects, segment them, and even automatically save them if you use Leadfuze!

All-in-all, I would recommend that you select something that provides most of the capabilities beyond just prospecting when searching for a sales prospecting automation tool, so that you do not have to invest in other tools separately. Originally, you might select a sales prospecting package that only provides sales prospecting and then, as your requirements expand, sign up for the same tool's higher price-more functionality package. Typically, this is how I go about it.

I hope I have given a full and detailed view of the resources I have mentioned above. Hopefully, based on my analysis and review, you will make a sound investment. Only write it in the comments, and I'll make sure I get in contact with you. Have more questions.

Questions related to the option of prospecting software for sales:

What is sales discovery, and how does it affect your company?

Sales prospecting is the system by which calls are made, and emails are sent to leads leading to conversion. It includes cold emailing, SMS, contacting people who may have gone cold and may be new to your product, or nurturing leads. As it helps to expand your business and meet potential customers, it is vital for your company.

What do tools for sales prospecting do with automation?

Sales prospecting tools with automation allow you to simplify the sales targeting processes. It helps to conduct all the activities associated with sales prospecting faster and with greater effectiveness. Mostly, these processes target redundant tasks.

How can one enhance their strategies for sales prospecting?

From the very beginning, one should develop sales prospecting strategies. For the sales prospecting schedule, do not wait for sales to go slow. Nurture your current relationships and make efforts to better understand your customers so that you can plan your next steps accordingly.

What are the 2020's Best Sales Prospecting Automation Tools?

LeadFuze, Prospect.io, and FindThatLead are some of the many popular automation tools for sales prospecting. LeadFuze is a pretty good sales prospecting tool, but the best one depends entirely on your requirements and budget. I would suggest investing in a tool beyond sales prospecting that offers more functionality.

Which are the free automation tools for sales prospecting?

No, you do not have any free-sales prospecting software. All instruments come with a free trial period, and you need to pick a plan that fits your needs accordingly.

How to automate my sales prospecting strategies?

To automate your sales prospecting strategies, you would need to invest in sales automation tools. The sales automation tools automate redundant processes and make sales prospecting simple, quick, and efficient.

2. Integrate the Software for Sales Automation

Take for instance you have selected a program for sales automation. In that case, you must ensure that it interacts with the rest of your stack of sales technology, including your CRM, calendar program, and email marketing platform.

It should be easy to combine your instruments. You'll enjoy native integrations with common CRMs such as Salesforce and HubSpot if you have chosen to use one of the automated prospecting software tools mentioned above. Email platforms such as MailChimp and GetResponse, and calendar applications such as Calendly, can also be easily connected via Zapier.

You can move on to phase three once your sales automation software and integrations are configured: automating initial communication.

3. Initial Contact Automation

Not a lead is a name and an email address. It's a start, but once they demonstrate some kind of interest in your business and the goods you offer, a contact can't be qualified as an actual lead, which means that you need to make contact through automatic emails.

There is certainly an art of producing effective cold email campaigns. Luckily, we have a few techniques to help ensure that your messages are opened, read, and replied to:

—Nail Your Subject Line: The most significant aspect of your cold email is this. After all, nothing else matters if a receiver reads your subject line and chooses not to open your mail. You missed the lead. So make sure your subject lines are personal and short. For instance, "Bill, are you able to spare 5 minutes?"

—Concise Your Messages: Your recipients are busy. Even if said stranger sells the biggest, business-boosting gadget on the planet, they don't have time to read long-winded emails from random strangers. So make sure that your emails are brief, preferably two to four phrases, or five phrases at most.

—Add Personalization Elements: Add personalization elements to your automatic emails wherever possible, so they don't sound like mass mailings. You can do this easily by referencing the name, organization, and industry of the recipient. All these items can be found and easily added by your sales prospecting software.

—Include a CTA: End a call to action with every message. By asking a simple question at the bottom of your emails, we suggest doing this, which works because we are all wired to respond to the things asked of us. Just remember that it is casual and non-committal to keep up. At this point, you are just attempting to start a conversation.

—Follow Up, Don't Forget: Finally, don't forget to automate multiple messages! Your prospects are busy, we'll say it again. Every day, they have tons of emails flooding their inboxes, and yours might slip through the cracks. You'll multiply your chances of getting a response by sending emails each week or so.

Automate them to send a preset interval within your sales automation tool or email marketing platform once your cold emails are written.

4. Qualify your leads and segment them

You've chosen your sales prospecting software at this point and integrated it with your other instruments. You have also crafted and automated your initial contact emails to be sent at specific intervals. Hopefully, you have received a lot of answers!

Our automated prospecting system's final step is to qualify your leads. We propose that all of your contacts be segmented into one of four boxes: "Sales Ready / Good Fit," "Sales Ready / Bad Fit," "Sales Unready / Good Fit," and "Sales Unready / Bad Fit."

The best leads, clearly, the ones you can spend the bulk of your time on, are those that fall into the category of "Sales Ready / Good Fit." Leads that are unready to sell but tend to be a good fit should be nurtured.

We should also note that you have to know who your ideal customer is in order to qualify them correctly. If your business does not yet have crystal-clear buyer personas, it becomes mission number one to build them!

If you know the benefits that you promise (and deliver), then you know who your target groups are. In the B2B sector, for example, the target group can be an industry or a specific country, and in the B2C sector it could be an age group (18-24 years old) or an interest group (gardeners).

However, target groups are very imprecise and large. That is why the idea of the Buyer Personas exists. Buyer Personas is a method to identify in much more detail the people you want to reach digitally. For the B2C sector, the Buyer Persona describes characteristics such as "rarely walks among people", "interested in facts and figures", "vegan" and "always vacationing in low mountain ranges". For the B2B sector, the Buyer Persona describes characteristics such as "very innovative", "informs himself mainly online" and "little risk awareness". This makes Buyer Personas a model of the ideal customer. Suppliers often have about four to five different buyer personas in a market segment.

How to craft meaningful buyer personas

Oliver, Lars, Nils. These would be good fictitious names for your Buyer Persona if it is a male buyer in the pharmaceutical industry in Germany over 50. Mira, Tara or Maya, on the other hand, are suitable for buyer personas described by a female marketing assistant of Indian IT service providers under 30. Names and avatars make it much easier to address the persona and think up your actions from her point of view.

The overall goal is to address the right potential customers. To achieve this, there is the concept of a buyer persona. The expression *persona* comes from the ancient Greek word for masques in theatre. All roles in a classic Greek drama had predefined set of properties. And so buyer persona is also meant as: a predefined set of properties of your ideal or average customer.

A buyer persona is the extension of the target group's idea. A classic target group in B2B marketing would be, for example, buyers from the pharmaceutical industry - in other words, a position description and an industry. But this is far too imprecise for digital marketing. That is why the buyer persona was developed. Initially, it always refers to one product or one service. The buyer persona thus includes industry, position, age, gender, interests, motives, or ideas. So, you can answer the question of what is important to this persona and what drives it.

Here is an example.

Viola Vargas. She is married, has two children and likes to travel with her family on vacation to very exotic places like Zambia or Indonesia. She is a technical buyer and sets a great store by her ability to discover innovations. She likes to eat meat, but only organic. Musically, she listens to everything that is electronically produced.

During our journey as customers until the decision for a certain product or service is made, we have various questions concerning the offer and the provider. And this is exactly what we use to address the questions of our potential customers in a targeted manner and thus become exciting and relevant.

Now we bring both together. We'll put the buyer personas over the phases of the customer journey. And then we clarify how the questions of the Buyer Persona (which we then answer with our content) actually change. For example, in our example "Mira", 30, assistant in an IT company in Mumbai, which is a buyer persona for a Software-as-a-Service (CRM) startup. Mira regularly looks for new solutions. In the first phase of "research", she only looks at whether a solution is relevant at all. To do this, she has questions about the features and whether the provider has experience in their industry. At this point, a white paper "How our features help the IT industry" would be relevant for her.

So you go through all phases of a typical customer journey and develop the questions your buyer persona has in each phase. This can be done in internal workshops; it would be perfect to ask the real customer what interests they had in which phase of their journey. By the way: This is a good reason to get in touch with a customer you have not talked to for a long time.

No doubt about it, when you automate sales prospecting, you will see a huge leap in sales team productivity and motivation. Naturally, these two things will lead to an increase in company revenue too! Just remember to follow our automated four-step system of prospecting:

1. First, pick the correct tools for sales automation.
2. Second, integrate your software for sales automation.
3. Third, initial contact automation.
4. And fourth, qualify your leads, and segment them.

Automating Cold Calls: Best Practices to Follow

Cold calling is a science that requires charisma with equal components, infrastructure streamlining, and a fair degree with persistence.

In the past, in the first phase of the process, cold calling was used. A salesperson would get a list of untargeted names (usually purchased) and check off the names until they reached someone willing to meet with them personally or on the phone. This philosophy accompanied the probability principle: one party must choose to meet for every 100 calls made. Although this can bring some appointments, you will accept that there is a lot of time lost following this procedure! Cold calling has morphed into the second level of the sales process today. The cold email begins today, with the ball rolling in the process. The salesperson will send the cold email to the decision-maker and then reply, forward, or withdraw the person's email. If the cold lead is interested in understanding more, they should have a moment to take the next move and meet, becoming more open and attentive to the meeting naturally.

Automating this method may be a brilliant way to enhance the amount of calls you try every day. Still, it ensures you have to work a little harder to appreciate your leads' time and dignity, while also giving them something of value.

When you indulge in your cold call automation, bear in mind these six tips to ensure that the human aspect is not lost in the shuffle.

1. Automating Lead Scoring, Prioritize the Calls

There are some resources at your disposal to help you prioritize which people you want to reach out to first, before you or your auto-dialer decides to access someone on your cold call list.

Managed correctly, this won't be as "cold" as you're used to when having a cold call. For example, your CRM could participate in lead scoring based on who submitted a feedback form, the degree to which a lead has engaged with your brand online (including social media), and whether they have attached products to their carts or made regular visits to your web assets.

It may be the first time they communicate personally with your organization's representative by the time you meet them with a "cold" call. But rating the leads in advance means that when touch is made, you have already piqued and gauged their curiosity, and have also ensured that you will not be strangers.

2. Select a power dialer and a predictive dialer between.

It is necessary to know the difference between these two kinds of software for cold call automation, and then wisely choose which one is right for your business. How are they different then? Here are the main distinctions:

- Predictive Dialers: Predictive dialers can be used concurrently by live operators using medium-sized or large phone lists, or by making calls on multiple phone lines. When a call is picked up on one of the wires, agents are alerted and are not slowed down by disconnected calls, response machines, or dial tones.

- Power Dialers: Power dialers vary, in that on a single line, they make calls to one phone number after another. There is no pause when human reactions are on the other end of the line. The agent will react automatically.

When it comes to using predictive dialers, there are certain rules for consumer safety in place. Companies, for example, do not lose more than 3% of their attempted calls. That means you need a big enough team in place that you can respond to 97% of connecting calls. Your prospect would hang up if any of your agents are busy at one time, and may potentially block or even report your number.

3. Don't forget Voicemail

Despite the number of firms and agents not making use of it, voicemail can be a helpful service. Every telephone owner gets their share of unsolicited calls, but that seems to be as far as things go, in most situations. A missed call, an unknown number, and no voicemail provides specifics about the call. And with little to show for the interference, it leaves the receiver feeling disappointed and maybe even insecure.

Consider how you could profit from employing a "voicemail drop" program. Instead of leaving unhelpful missed call alerts on people's home screens, you can pick from pre-recorded voice messages and "kick" your message into the voicemail inbox of your prospect if a call does not go through.

Using a service like this would not guarantee a callback, but it has the power to provide value and an opportunity to get back in touch with the receiver of your call.

4. Record or transcribe automatically - and then evaluate your calls

Learning to communicate comfortably with others may feel like a lifetime pursuit for individuals who earn their living on the call. So, searching for call management tools or a different app that helps you record or transcribe your phone calls while you make them might make sense.

What's the value of this? For one thing, it helps you look back on your most successful calls and see what went well and what tactics and talking points in the future you should deploy again. To gather any data that you may have skipped, you will also be able to go back to the transcript.

The value for your call receivers is clear: they get to work with a telephone agent that is devoted to enhancing their attitude, their product expertise, and their ability to walk the fine line between moving ahead to a good transaction while also keeping a "distance" that is polite and coolly helpful.

5. Choose the best platforms to track the leaders and cultivate them.

The ingredient your marketing team has been lacking might be following up on a cold call with another form of touch. So, what's the right way for this to happen? We know calling and emailing with a lot of trial and error is always the most effective mix of outreach forms. Here's what we understand:

Companies who use email after a cold call to follow up on their leads are 16 percent more likely to receive an answer.

If enterprises use personalized text messaging rather than emails, they are 40 percent more likely to convert.

Companies who utilize new platforms for lead nurturing see 9% more salespeople meeting their quotas efficiently.

Even after your cold call has finished, social media is a means to cultivate your leads and offer added value and perspectives.

6. Offer something of worth away

Cold calling is always cold calling, no matter how artfully you do it or how robust the CRM you use to get it done. If your power dialer gets the interesting "Hello?" on the other end of the line, your agents need to deliver something of worth. Your leaders would like to know that their time is not taken for granted, which means providing free value for anything.

It's the same idea that governs content marketing on the internet. If you ask someone to do something, such as sign up for your mailing list or follow up on a deal on your website, they often require a subtle push. That drive can come in the form of quality content such as a video created professionally, a whitepaper with convincing analysis and case studies, a product and service preview or tutorial, or something else from your concept.

Providing something valuable for the leaders, whether in the B2B or B2C culture, helps create connections and launch a discussion. It is a "way in" to chat about the advantages of your offering. Still, it also expresses how much you respect your leaders' time and appreciate their desires or their business model, if appropriate.

Automate Followup Emails

You've got a new contact. A new client. A Fresh Lead. This is the time when someone is most interested in what you have to say.

When people want to hear from you.

An effective follow-up sequence is a key strategy for your business. And it becomes much more productive when you can automate the sequence.

It runs once you set it up—and nurtures leads into clients without any extra work.

Usage of predefined rules to trigger email messages based on clients taking certain acts or not taking them. Some examples include a welcome email sent when a customer signs up for a mailing list, or a brief notification that something was put by the customer in their cart, but never completed checking out. Email automation takes simple work off your to-do list to free up your time for many other essential activities, such as response to customer questions. It can help clients learn more about your brand, inspire them to keep coming back, or remind them in the first place why they purchased from you.

You'd like to remain linked to your clients as a marketer or company owner. Email automation is a versatile instrument that helps you to deliver the right message at the right time to the right people.

Email automation is a way to produce emails at the right moment that hit the right people with the right message, without doing the job at all times.

You can target individuals based on actions, interests, and previous sales when you connect your website analytics with your email marketing platform. Then you can personalize the experience of each customer and increase your messaging 's importance.

Recipe #3 Auto follow-up fair or event leads

Ingredients: A business card scanner app on your phone (or might even be your CRM's app that is capable of scanning business cards)

Method: Have you ever spent hours in the evening after an exhausting day at a fair stand? Instead of going swimming or doing some yoga to relax? The good news: These times are over, forever. You just need the time to scan the business cards and send the data to your CRM. What is your main sales goal at that fair or event? You write the follow-up email pointing your prospect to the correspondent CTA. And you setup the process: A) for new scanned business cards B) send out this email sequence. And you are done!

Difficulty: Intermediate.

Purpose: Save you tons of time following up the same kind of prospect.

Total time: 2 hours.

THE ADVANTAGES OF Email AUTOMATION

Automation of email lets you:

1. Personalize the interactions of your clients.

Research backs up what most advertisers already know: consumers love personalization.

90 % of customers find personalized content somewhat attractive.

91% of customers are more likely to patronize companies that have reviews and deals that are individualized.

A recent experiment showed that their click-through rates increased by 11 percent, and revenue from the product increased by 38 percent when shoppers learned an ad was focused on their behavior on the platform.

72 percent of clients only respond to marketing messages that target their interests in 2019.

Email is the leading form of personalization experience used by marketers.

To help build your relationships with your clients and your company, you can even create a series of automated emails.

2. Make the most of your squad of marketers.

Automation is transforming the way that all sorts of teams conduct business. According to a 2017 survey of information staff, respondents said they think it would increase the productivity of employees:

69% said automation could help minimize the time lost.

59% said that if their work's repetitive aspects are automated, they could save at least 6 hours a week.

72% said they would use the time they saved to concentrate on work of greater importance.

For instance, this may mean less time spent on assembling email lists and scheduling messages manually for email marketing teams. Alternatively, team members may use the opportunity to concentrate on other significant activities, such as in-depth customer relationship building.

The bottom line: Everything is achieved with automation, and the additional efficiency is of greater benefit.

3. Boost the rate of customer retention.

Selling to a current client is much faster and more cost-effective than transforming a new one, and you can keep in touch longer than ever with automation. Schedule your messages so that without hearing from you, your customers don't go waiting for too long, and make sure the copy is necessary to maximize its impact.

An email that reads, "Hey, in a while, we haven't heard from you. Pay us a visit!" has a very high possibility of ending up in the garbage. Only compare it to this one:

"We haven't heard from you in a while, dear Joe, and we wanted to make sure you heard about our latest deal. A new model came out of the printer you've been buying parts for, and it's 20 percent off! Come check it out."

This is an example of a message satisfying a need that is more likely to attract a customer back.

4. It makes the strategy of marketing scalable.

When you manually send out an email set, your staff's size limits the number of clients you can meet. If your customer base unexpectedly doubled in size, will you be able to remain on schedule? What if it had tripled?

Automation makes the marketing of email scalable. When you've set it up in such a way that every time someone signs up for your mailing list your website sends a message, you don't have to make sure a staff member is available to do it.

With email automation, as soon as they perform some of the acts you monitor, clients automatically integrate into your system. Without extra demands on your limited resources, their behavior tells your machine what messages to send them next.

The use of email automation to expand your company

A trigger in email automation is a particular date, occurrence, or action of a contact that tells the device to send a related message. Based on your contact's journey, you can select triggers and activated messages.

To get you started, here are a few examples:

Trigger: New subscriber

Email: "Welcome!"

And if an e-commerce store is your website, many of your first-time visitors won't be prepared to make a purchase. What do you do with an email once you have it to catch their attention with a 'subscribe now' button?

Following a work interview, welcome emails have been like thank you cards. There is no law that you must give them, but when you don't, people notice:

74% of individuals expect a welcome email to be received when they subscribe to a mailing list.

Welcome messages receive four times more readings and five times more clicks than regular marketing newsletters.

They produce per email as much as 320% more revenue than other promotional messages.

Following up with a warm welcome will help transform new leads into customers without any additional effort when you get a new subscriber.

Trigger: Abandonment of carts

"Email: "Forget something?"

Adding an item to your cart only takes one press, but following through takes more steps. For many reasons, including having to register for an account's high shipping costs, as well as osite's security protocol of the site, about 70 percent of e-commerce shoppers abandon their carts.

Abandoned emails from carts can help you restore lost sales. You can start regaining your shoppers' interest once you get to know your audience and write a clear, timely email.

Trigger: New products or promotions

Email: "For you, something special!"

Your messages can begin to lose their effectiveness if you announce every new product release, upgrade, or promotion to every customer.

Email automation helps you avoid this trap because, based on their interests, it allows you to announce products to specific customers. In reality, you can increase revenue per email opening by an average of 150 percent, if you provide customized suggestions in your email campaign.

MAKING THE AUTOMATION OF EMAIL MORE EFFICIENT

Here are some tips to help your newly automated email strategy run smoothly:

1. To gather more information, monitor responses.

You have the chance to get key details from each client every time you send an automatic email. You will learn whether or not the person:

- Opens the email
- Clicks through to your site
- Uses an offer
- Buys a product proposed
- Continues browsing once they're on your site

Everything you learn about your shoppers can guide your next move when targeting your automated emails. Try a different tactic if your recipients do not open your coupon emails or click on your suggestions.

2. strategically offer discounts.

One of the main reasons why people leave their shopping carts is the high cost of shipping.

You can't remove shipping costs or lower your rates, but you can send out discount coupons or promo codes to draw reluctant spenders. It can be an efficient approach, but be careful not to overuse it. Your customers might start to think they are entitled to receiving them more frequently if you give too many discounts.

3. Develop drip campaigns that are automated.

Many individuals connect with your business several times until they become clients. Drip campaigns "drip" useful content about a company, product, or industry gradually.

These campaigns have to be specific to function, and drip campaign messages only go out to prospects who have shown interest through email automation.

Start to create client relationships

Automation of emails lets you find your audience and engage your clients. Automations run in the background instead of manual campaigns, as you attend to other precious activities.

You can send customized emails to each customer via automation, from new visitors to repeat buyers. And you can refine your targeting every time you send a message and develop your company without losing the unique personal touch if you combine email automation with customer analytics.

Your follow-up sequence needs to be strategic, whether you are in the process of developing the first follow-up sequence or you have been at this for years.

It should be the product of a concrete strategy designed to accomplish a particular purpose.

Unfortunately, to fill in gaps, follow-up is often generated on a whim, or pieced together bit by bit over time. This implies that most sequences are not generated to achieve specific results and do not actually accomplish much of anything.

Importantly, a lot has changed since you created your sequences.

There are powerful new tools for marketing out there. You know more about your clients. Your product line has changed, or you have learned more about effective online marketing.

It's necessary to update your follow-up sequence. This chapter is about how to re-imagine your follow-up and incorporate everything that you have not gotten to but should.

Your follow-up is begging to be updated

(but your website gets all the attention)

Your automated follow-up is your online marketing's neglected workhorse, which is a shame because it is one of the most effective resources at your disposal, and it will be encountered by almost all your leads and clients.

We are fascinated with the smallest details of our website and could go for months without even thinking about our automated marketing follow-up.

Your automated follow-up brings contacts back to your site day in and day out, creates a bond with them, produces and nurtures professional leads, drives conversions, contributes to customer loyalty, and saves you untold time.

Automation is one of the easiest ways to follow up with clients, so the time it would take to make it better to do all of this stuff is definitely worth it.

What follows is a seven-step process that will create a specific follow-up plan for your company. Make sure that you automate and achieve as much as possible, and that you enhance the overall experience for your contacts.

Any time you spend on this will pay dividends, as each new contact experiences your automated follow-up. You're not really wasting time at all; you're investing it in one of the highest leverage activities in your organization/business.

Here are the steps you need:

1. Get a fresh start
2. Pick your destination
3. Know what you will do along the way
4. Get there "by..."
5. Map it out
6. Make a plan
7. Learn from where you've been

Get a fresh start

Forget your old follow-up sequences in order to build a new and enhanced strategy. Set them aside mentally and start over with a new outlook.

We are shooting for a complete, "top to bottom" overhaul of your automated follow-up. Adding to what exists would only lead to gradual changes.

Instead, to accomplish a big leap in performance, we will create something completely fresh and inspired.

Pick your destination

We will establish two different follow-up sequences; one for our prospects and one for our clients, because after their first purchase, our emphasis changes.

At that point, we switch from helping a contact understand why they should do business with us; from building trust and educating them, to customer support, encouraging repeat purchases, and getting referrals.

As you develop your new follow up plan, you want to be guided by a clear vision of the perfect experience you want each contact to have before and after they make a purchase.

This "perfect" client experience is not going to happen on its own ... by envisioning it, describing it, and then working towards it, we're going to make it happen.

So imagine the perfect experience that you want each contact to have, then build a brief description explaining the experience that you want them to have as a prospect, and then build the experience that you want them to have as a client.

Keep these descriptions short (two to three sentences, tops). Striving for a multi-faceted experience is okay, but don't go overboard. Focus on only a handful of crucial things that you want to get out of your marketing follow-up.

This is not making a plan. It is just choosing a destination, so you can be confident you will end up where you want to be.

Think of this as the mission statement for your automated follow-up marketing—it should be inspirational, but not specific.

Here's an instance of how yours might look:

As a prospect:

- I want to "surprise my new contact from the very moment they confirm their subscription. I want to provide great content so that they are excited to see emails from me. I want them to think of me as an ally, friend, and expert.

As a customer:

- I want to provide my clients with such excellent service that they feel obliged to share our website with their family and friends, do not hesitate to buy again, and do not consider using another company.

When you are satisfied that you have captured the importance of the experience you are striving for, move on to the next step...

Know what you will do along the way

If the summary statement you just developed is your destination, we can now pick all the things you will get done en route.

Really spend some time considering... "Ideally, what would my automated follow-up do for me?"

Would you like your automated follow-up to:

- Create trust?
- Strengthen your relationship with prospects?
- Increase referrals?
- Increase repeat visits?

- Reduce refunds?
- Educate on benefits?
- Create testimonials and review?
- Collect feedback and experiences?
- Establish you as an authority?
- Encourage upgrading?
- Describe available product options?
- Increase order frequency?
- Create more affiliates and resellers?
- Increase your social media following?
- Increase order size?
- Position you as "best of breed?"
- Increase big ticket backend sales?
- Turn customers into evangelists?
- Increase engagement?
- Reduce customer support requests?
- Shorten the buying cycle?
- Make repeat sales?
- Identify and assign "hot leads?"
- Educate on industry?
- Develop a community?

This is where you choose the outcomes that your follow-up creates, so take your time.

These goals should not be particular or measurable. In fact, it is better if they aren't. We're just making a list of wishes. We will concentrate on how you will accomplish these goals in the next phase, and then we will make them specific and measurable.

Don't think about how you're going to do all of this, at least not yet. That will only stifle your imagination and reduce your ambition needlessly. Instead, without restricting yourself to what is feasible or realistic, concentrate on what you would like to do.

Write them down in a large, unorganized list as ideas come to you — the more ambitious the list, the better. Stretch the boundaries of what is achievable, so that you create an automatic sequence of follow-ups that does everything it can for you and your contacts.

When your list is done, let's organize it a bit...

Separate the objectives by whether they are prospect (pre-sale) or consumer (post-sale). Put them as well as you can in chronological order (you probably won't be able to do this perfectly).

So, your list might look like this:

Goals for prospect follow-up:
- Establish value proposition
- Position us as the premier solution
- Segment by product interest
- Segment contacts by persona
- Assign top leads to salespeople
- Get contacts back to website

Goals for customer follow-up:
- Motivate them to upgrade their order
- Give a free gift as a "thank you"
- Send postcard in mail with a client discount code
- Collect testimonials and reviews
- Measure customer satisfaction
- Encourage referrals and word of mouth
- Increase frequency and repeat orders

If you feel you have completed this step, check your objectives against the experience you have defined. Are enough of these goals based on the client and creating an amazing experience for them?

You are ready to move on to the next step if you feel your priorities reflect the needs of your organization and the needs of your contacts.

Get there "by..."

It's time to get the rubber closer to the road now that you know what you want to do. Link methods to each objective by completing a "by ..." statement:

"Increase engagement" by...

- Emailing new blog articles
- Asking what content they would want
- Incentivizing social media follows

"Increase repeat sales" by...

- Sending info on rewards program
- Providing 'client only' discount (20%?)
- Notify of bi-weekly sales

"Increase order size" by...

- Sending a 'one click upgrade' offer instantly
- Purchase-one-get-one offer on accessories
- Suggest complimentary products

Put a lot of time into brainstorming all the ways in which you could achieve these objectives. Again, don't restrict yourself to what you think is possible, because some of your best ideas will needlessly wall you off. Just list every idea you have about how you can achieve a goal.

Don't stop pushing yourself if you've got 3-5 good ideas. Your first five ideas will be very safe, and probably stuff you've been considering anyway.

Do not stop there. Push yourself well beyond this point.

Numbers 17 and 31 may be your best ideas, but if you stop at number 5, you will never find them.

If you do it right, this phase will generate some of the best ideas for developing your business you've had in a long time. Highlight the most brilliant thoughts you've come up with.

Map it out

Pen and paper may be the perfect way to work out the first few drafts when it comes to laying out the exact follow-up email sequence. Just make sure you have plenty of paper.

There are going to be false starts, arrows that go nowhere, cross-outs, and scribbles.

That is what you want.

If this is simple, and you're not confused about how all this is going to come together, you may need to back up and try the steps again, because you might not have been ambitious enough.

This should feel like putting together a puzzle - you have the pieces and now you are trying to find out how they fit together so that they lead prospects through the phases of the purchasing cycle and solidify your relationship with your clients.

Don't get caught up in the specifics; you can worry about the settings needed, or the subject lines for your emails later on. Only scribble out the overall method and get down to the basic sequence of events.

If you get a flash of insight, maybe make some notes. However, you can fill in most of the details later ... this is still the "big picture" moment.

Try out our automation builder when it's time to fine tune the marvelous follow-up sequence that is emerging. If you've used it, you know it's a tool that's surprisingly quick to use. It's as simple as reading a flowchart to map out a marketing automation sequence.

The objectives of the sequence will differ depending on your business model, but generally speaking, make sure that your follow-up marketing offers content that is:

- Positioning you as "best of breed".
- Communicating the value you provide.
- Differentiating you from the competition.
- Delivering as much value as possible.
- Establishing trust and nurturing a relationship.
- Educating your prospect with knowledge they will need to make an informed decision when it comes time to buy.

You will want to distribute these messages all through your automated marketing sequences.

Sadly, your prospect is not paying attention to everything you say, so you will need to be somewhat repetitive to ensure they hear your core marketing messages.

Don't be afraid to repeat yourself on crucial points, so you can be sure that even though they skipped part of your email sequence, your prospect receives the right message.

Make a plan

Once you feel satisfied that your follow-up marketing ideas accomplish the vision you created in "Step 2: Decide where you are going" and the objectives you created in "Step 3: Know what you will do along the way," it is time to get the ball rolling.

Make a list of what you need to create to make this happen.

It is probably going to be mostly content that you need to make, such as emails or free reports, but you may also need to plan new projects, such as developing a refer-a-friend program, developing a "one-click upsell" script, or some graphic design work you need to outsource.

Using a project management program may be useful, so that you can break it down to actionable plan and allocate the resources needed for each project.

Learn from where you've been

In order to introduce your new automated follow-up strategy, it will possibly take a while to ensure that you have mined your old follow-up sequence for all the knowledge it contains before switching over.

If you haven't already, define key indicators that you can use to assess your marketing success in order to compare the new and old email follow-up sequences.

This new approach for follow-up could work better than your old one. However, you want to be able to develop that as a fact. You can only do that if you know the numbers.

Some useful metrics:

- Unsubscription rate

- Traffic referred by email
- Open rate
- Link clicks
- Average time to purchase
- Average lead score
- Sales referred by email
- Deals that are added / time
- Number of leads / time

Make sure to set up our Google Analytics integration if you haven't already, so that you can track link clicks in specific automations and emails.

You will also see how contacts interact with your website and know what "goals" your marketing automation and email marketing are responsible for.

While you are thinking it terms of analytics, find out how you will measure performance for all the goals created in Step 2, and the individual components of your email sequence created in Step 3.

Establish the basic metrics that are key to indicating performance and set up a schedule to review and analyze the various components of your follow-up, so that before the next full reconsideration it will continue to advance.

If you repeat this process every year, you can keep developing experimental sequences to beat the output of your proven "control" sequence via email and other marketing channels.

That way, you will continue to challenge your best work and continuously aspire for that ultimate, unbeatable sequence of follow-up that automates as much of your business as possible and produces happy, pleased customers from your leads.

Automate Workflows

Recipe #4 Automate workflow with sales reps

Ingredients: A shared sheet (with Google, Dropbox or Microsoft), a glue service as Zapier or Automate.io, Email marketing tool or CRM

Method: This one is to streamline cold calling processes. I have a sales rep who is doing the cold calls for me. Both of us work on the same sheet. I put in the new potentials. And the sales rep gets the names from there and calls. If the potential is interested, the rep just puts in their email addresses in a specific column ("Information via email") of that sheet. Then there is an automation which checks that column and assigns that potential to a specific email sequence. By the way: There is another column for those who want a personal phone call with me ("Phone call"). These potentials are assigned to another email sequence sending out my Calendly link to them.

Difficulty: Advanced.

Purpose: To streamline cold calling.

Total time: One day.

Part III: This is Social Selling Automation

Why Use Social Automation?

"The more I learn about people, the more I like my dog. "

- Mark Twain

You know: Interacting on social media is important. It brings you leads and enhances your reputation. But …. it is so time consuming. Finding blitz content that engages, viewing all posts of your network, let alone commenting on them. Don´t worry, there is a solution to this dilemma.

Automation of social media means the use of resources and algorithms to automate or semi-automate the process of content creation, uploading, and sharing on social networks such as Twitter, Instagram and LinkedIn. With one tool, you can also simplify parallel operations on multiple networks. It's one main part of marketing automation as a whole.

By automating some of your company's social media activities with social media automation tools, you can ensure that you stay active across your social accounts without being forced to update and post in real-time. For me it is honestly quite like magic what I have discovered about this.

Today, social media marketing is everything. Having an active profile on social media can help you associate your company with consumers, improve your brand's exposure, increase your revenue, and assist you with customer acquisition.

It's time to get fully on board that social media hype train along with everyone else and their grandmas. With this handy guide, you'll find out exactly what you need in order to perfect your social media shenanigans.

To kick things off, let's start with a simple question: Why should you care about social media automation in the first place? Let's run through a few explanations and helpful illustrations.

Push the Website with targeted traffic

You can choose what information to display to a single customer with social network automation, based on their previous actions, desires, and much more.

This will help direct traffic to your website in exchange. With a single click, consumers interested in your content will switch seamlessly from social media sites to your website. And hopefully, transform, transform.

Boost the SEO of Your Website

Evergreen content is SEO content that remains popular and can be reposted over time without losing its relevance across social networks. It contains relevant keywords from search engines such as Google that drive search traffic.

Furthermore, evergreen content generates traffic from other websites linking to your domain. Yep, that's right: other people are more likely to connect to your posts for SEO purposes when you produce a high-quality, evergreen piece of content that people would love to read and post on social media.

Understanding the desires & wishes of your customers

A massive volume of data on their followers is gathered from social media sites. You can exploit this knowledge with analytics software to give the consumers the kind of content they're interested in.

You can quickly track hashtags, likes, and reshares, for instance, to decide how your content resonates with your clients. Although likes would not give you a lot of insight into what consumers are converting, it's a simple way to figure out whether your content is important or not.

Building The Brand

Brand recognition should be one of the top priorities for every company, since it 1) establishes a reputation that lets you get to know and trust your clients, and 2) differentiates you from your rivals.

Successful engagement on social media will assist with brand creation, as individuals who don't even follow you will be introduced across multiple channels to your content. If that content is relevant to them, they'll soon trust your brand to create and share high-quality content consistently. And you'll be at the top of their mind when they're ready to buy.

Paid Advertising

A major chunk of social media content is not as readily accessible as before, thanks to algorithms. Today, paid advertisements are also an excellent way to target a broader audience, and social media management platforms and systems are the perfect way to run targeted ads.

In addition, many sites (including Facebook Market Manager, Twitter Ads Manager, LinkedIn Ads) have paid advertisement programs that you can use to target and reach specific customers.

The ROI on advertising on social media can be humongous. By comparing how much you spent on paying social advertisements, in comparison to how many leads or purchases you receive from social media marketing, you can calculate it effectively.

Acquire new customers

By using social media automation instruments to target customers who suit your ideal consumer profile (ICP), you can quickly meet high-quality prospects that are not yet familiar with your brand.

Make sure guests can quickly click on your content straight from the social media platform on your website. This way, the transfer is as simple as possible until someone discovers your brand or product.

Generate More Sales

Marketing on social media allows you to connect quickly with your followers and target and influence your clients, all of which will make you happier in the long run, and will get you paying customers.

Keep your presence on Social Media consistent.

Many automation systems help you plan when to post content. They plan ahead of time for your social media activity, maintaining consistency in your scheduling.

The most appropriate hours for posting to various sites are different times of the day. You will build and find the content beforehand and time it to be released automatically, instead of making the marketing staff members manually click the "publish" button at precisely the right times.

There are also lots of instruments that will help you find important content to share and when to share it. Later, we'll dig through those cool apps; however, News.me, for instance, lists all the stories most often shared with your Facebook or

Twitter friends, which you can also then post, trusting that your friends will like to read it.

Save A Lot Of Time

It takes several hours to manually build, publish and distribute content in real-time across all your social media channels. These hours could be put to good use for other things, such as preparing your campaign and ensuring that all your content is of high quality. The automation of social media plays the role of a time saver.

Automation of social media also allows you and your social media staff more time to spend on answering one-on-one questions, tweets, and remarks. And that's precisely how you build a true bond with your audience.

Gain more control of your strategy on social media

The type of content you upload, the day you post it (you can plan updates and articles for weekends or in the middle of the night if you feel like it), your sharing frequency, and your presence on various sites at once can be easily managed through social media automation.

It is way too time-intensive to take care of all these boring activities personally. Once your social media messages are automated, precisely when you have timed them, they will be sent out, which lets you monitor and evaluate your social marketing results.

21% of people unfollow brands that post redundant or bland stuff, 19% unfollow too much (6 + times a day) brands that post. Aggressive behavior and material contrary to the brand are other primary factors to obey.

Measure the social media accounts' success

When you automate the social networking shenanigans, the social interaction (likes, reshares, etc.) the content gets on multiple social media sites can be conveniently tracked, and the plan modified accordingly.

You should find out what metrics (likes, reshares, lead gen, sales?) are applicable to you and carefully track them within one method. All the analytics then assist you with your social media marketing plan to understand whether you're doing right or wrong.

If something doesn't work, depending on real statistics and not just best guesses, you should take the appropriate steps to optimize it.

Mastering Social Media In 3 Simple Measures

I use a lot of social automation. In recent years I tried a lot of things, but not all of them worked quite well. Here is what I learned. To accomplish your goals & create a following, employ these three moves:

1. Know What (And When) to automate

Automate and recycle the evergreen material of your own (and others') between new entries. Your social media profile should be constant (which means that you should write regularly) because it is futile to produce new material from scratch every day.

Content curation, or stealing from people that have already done the job for you by making it, is something you can easily do. There are many fascinating things out there. Download and recycle the evergreen content if it makes sense. Apply one of these strategies or both of them.

Analytics tools will inform you when your followers are online and connect with you to schedule the updates at the proper hours. Only remember to pay attention to distinctive time zones.

This was already mentioned, but I'll say it again because it's crucial: Don't automate human interactions. Ever. Do you know what's not a good look? Sending out spammy, automated DMs, or replies.

Here's a real-life example: When American Airlines merged with US Airways, they created an automated thank you message on Twitter to be sent out each time someone mentioned them, assuming these mentions would be positive. This backfired with unhappy customers who tagged them with something entirely different from a "thank you" in mind.

2. Ensure that all your content on social media is relevant

Make sure that the content for the brand and target demographic is still important. This also suggests that you can only publish the best quality content. Make sure that the headline is still personalized to suit and channel while curating and recycling material from other creators. Anything that looks amazing on LinkedIn may not work on Instagram.

Use analytics tools to know what traffic content draws and what it doesn't. Figure out what's doing well with your social media followers and users interacting with your brand.

And here's just one more free tip: Don't be too salesy.

A successful way to stop this is to follow the 411 social media concept, which means that you write four original posts, one recycled or chosen post, and one self-promotional post for each set of social media messages. That one self-promotional post is where you get to tell everyone why your item is better than its rivals.

3. Choose the Best Tools for the Best Channels

In just a second, we'll get to those resources, but let's briefly explore why. Why not just post your well-performing piece of content in any single medium of social media?

The reality is that since individuals use multiple social media platforms for radically different reasons, the same ideas are not going to work everywhere. Depending on your social media approach, pick your fights, and use analytics to see what specifically works better for your company.

Also, scheduling the same social media posts for all platforms is not a good idea. To suit each different platform, always curate and edit your content. The post itself and headings, CTAs, photos, etc. are included in this.

Automation Software for Social Media For Different Sites

You might try things like IFTTT or Zapier in order to make the various platforms you are using speak to each other and function together as smoothly as possible.

IFTTT (If This, Then That) is a plugin that helps all your apps work together with certain predefined triggers quite seamlessly, so you can retweet something based on hashtags automatically.

In certain ways, Zapier is a close approach. Once anyone responds on a Facebook post, you can get your email app to send automatic emails, and have all the related information in your CRM in no time.

Although there are lots of various applications and automation solutions for social media management of specific channels out there, here is a short guide to some of the better ones.

Twitter Workflow software

You could try something like Buffer to automate your Twitter account, which is designed to automatically post your tweets and suggest the best times to do so.

Crowdfire is another handy app that helps you identify inactive users and include analytics software. It also shares cross-platform content and recommends optimal posting times on each one of them.

Facebook Automation tools

Hootsuite sponsors all the main social media sites. You can follow analytics quickly, produce data, use an automated search feature, and plan posts and responses. Buzzsumo, which helps you search for related content and filter outcomes based on the venue, category, site, and so on, is quite fascinating.

LinkedIn Automation software

Big, fat warning: Some of the ideas introduced here may really cause Linkedin closing your account forever. You will have to do this at your own risk.

The terms of use of LinkedIn are tight, and they don't encourage automation of too many operations, so it's a safe idea to do it in moderation and stick to supported plugins.

Dux-Soup is a helpful lead generation plugin: affirm your links' expertise, subscribe to alerts, and send custom photos. But you can do it safely and according to the user agreement, as LinkedIn says on their webpage as well.

I work a lot with LinkedHelper. There are more than a dozen handy features in it and I love them all. In the new version 2, you can setup campaigns with workflows. This looks more or less like the following recipe.

Recipe #5 Connecting with a lot of new contacts at LinkedIn

Ingredients: A tool like LinkedHelper or Expandi

Method: With a tool, it is really easy to connect with a lot of people. Here is the way it goes: First you search on LinkedIn for your buyer persona (for example: CEO machinery Florida). You tell the tool to put the search results in a list. Next step is to create a compelling message. Need inspiration? "Hi Jane, It would be awesome if you accepted my invite. Warm regards, Tim" (instead of Jane, you put the names variable here). And now comes the magic: You tell the tool to automatically visit the profiles collected earlier and connect to each and every one of them using your prebuilt message. And off we go. There is a limit restriction in the tools, at around 100 contacts per day. Don´t overwrite it. You can define a reply for the contacts that answer you. In my case, this would be something like "Thank you Jane for connecting. Maybe sales automation becomes a topic of interest for you in the future. Warm regards, Tim". *Why I don´t send her a pitch right away?* This is seen as sleazy by most people on LinkedIn (including me).

Difficulty: Beginner.

Purpose: Get in contact with new potentials.

Total time: 2 hours.

Attention: DISCLAIMER: This is really important. You will do this at your own risk. I have heard of people banned by LinkedIn for doing this.

But there is more you could do with LinkedHelper. You can autovisit profiles (based on interests), automatically endorse your contacts (and hoping that they endorse you back) and you can auto-follow contacts.

You can also auto-scrape your contacts' data, (more on this in the next recipe.)

Beside LinkedHelper there are more tools doing the job as Expandi, Zopto or ProspectIn.

A slightly different type of automation comes with Phantombuster. With this one, you can automate LinkedIn, Twitter and Instagram tasks just with the ones mentioned above. But you can also auto-comment on posts. The difference lies in the pricing: You pay for the features you use (they call it Phantoms).

Recipe #6: Scraping your LinkedIn contacts and reaching out with email.

Ingredients: LinkedIn account with serious number of relevant contacts, scraper tool like LinkedHelper, and an email marketing solution (as Convertkit, HubSpot or EngagementBay).

Method: You collect potentials as new contacts in LinkedIn. Then you start LinkedHelper to scrape their contact data. This may take a while, since there is a restriction of a maximum of 150 contacts per day. LinkedHelper puts them all in a csv sheet. You can export this sheet afterwards to your email marketing solutions and send out semi-cold emails to this contacts. You might make reference to your connection on LinkedIn. And what works best is not a salesy email but just a question such as "Hi John, I wonder if you might be interested in sales automation at your company. Would be marvelous if you could point me in the right direction. Warm regards, Tim".

Difficulty: Intermediate

Purpose: To intensify contact with potentials.

Total time: To set it up 4 hours, extraction of data depending on the amount of contacts you have.

Attention: Do not use this one for potentials in the EU, as it is not GDPR compliant.

And now the last one: LinkedHub.

This does a great job. In a specific profile on LinkedIn, you can tell this Chrome extension to synchronize your HubSpot with this profile´s contact data. And the best: This doesn't even have to be your contact.

YouTube Automation tools

Tools like Jarvee help build your YouTube channel (and others like Pinterest, Tumblr, and Facebook) by following related influencers and profiles, and thereby giving your company visibility if you want to step up your YouTube game.

Another device that lets you keep track of what's going on with your channel is Senator, and it also provides support with auto-subscription and other platforms for auto-linking.

Instagram Automation Tools

Instagram has plenty of valuable software for automation. You can check it out later to arrange and prepare the look of your business's Instagram feed and Instagram stories, or try SocialCaptain, an AI module that distributes content to your ideal clients and automatically recalibrates its targeting, depending on your account interaction.

Understanding Social Selling

Why you should care, and how to do it properly is what it is.

Social selling is a modern selling technique that enables salespeople to target their prospecting laser-target and build relationships across established ties.

Selling socially. You've probably heard of it by now, but you might not be sure what it means.

Is it the same as ads on social media? (No.)

What about exposure to social media? (Nope, that's completely something else.)

Social selling enables salespeople to target laser customers, build relationships with their networks, and maybe even dismiss the dreaded cold calling practice.

You're probably already losing customers to more socially savvy peers if you have not yet integrated social selling into your funnel. But once you're done reading this chapter, that's going to change.

Let's get there.

What do social sales mean?

Social selling is the art of communicating, discovering, knowing, and cultivating sales prospects using social media. It's the latest way of building positive relationships with potential buyers, because when they're ready to buy, you're the first person or brand a prospect thinks about.

It has replaced the dreaded cold calling method for many salespeople, and the majority of our customers exhale with relief.

You are still interested in social selling fundamentals if you have a Facebook Business Page, LinkedIn profile, or a professional Twitter account, even if you have never really used the word to describe your online activities or thought too much about exactly what social selling entails.

To understand what social selling means, it is perhaps equally essential to explain what social selling is not. With unsolicited tweets and private messages, it's not about bombarding strangers. For that, there's a name: spam. And it shouldn't be done by us.

Social selling is about developing relationships and listening for the right moment to join the conversation so that you can introduce yourself as a solution to a dilemma, not just about getting access to contacts. The goal is to resolve an urgent need to make your prospect's life easier, instead of being yet another irritant to neglect online.

Now that you know what social selling is, let's look at why your organization needs to do it well.

THREE REASONS WHY THE COMPANY SHOULD BE INVOLVED IN SOCIAL SALES

In this next segment, you'll read many statistics, as we look at why your brand should care about the social sale. But really, there's one large 800-pound gorilla that cares for a reason: social sales works.

In reality, 78% of salespeople participating in social selling outsell their peers who do not.

If your sales team has not adopted social selling, your sales are simply not what they should be. Here are three essential explanations of why.

1. Your sales team can build a real relationship with social selling

Let's face it: no one wants to make cold calls. And the fact is that it's not very effective anyway: 90% of top decision-makers say they never respond to cold calls. Using social tools to listen to market-relevant conversations, known as social listening, helps the sales team identify potential leads who are already talking about the business, your rivals, or your market. When the time is right, you can hit them slowly with valuable information.

One in three B2B professionals said in a recent survey by CSO Insights and Seismic, that social selling tools increased the number of leads they had to deal with. Moreover, 39% said that social tools decreased the amount of time they spent investigating accounts and contacts.

Instead of being intrusive and cold, your first point of contact can be personalized, relevant, and helpful, with prospects socially sharing so much data on their public profiles about their needs, wants, and pain points. With 31 percent of B2B professionals saying that social selling tools allowed them to develop deeper relationships with consumers, this can lead to more essential ongoing opportunities and customer interaction.

Better still, developing a strong network across different social media platforms enables you to seek out introductions across established mutual connections to new sales opportunities, creating an instant sense of confidence and partnership. For both consumers and salespeople, the confidence is an extremely valuable resource, with 87 percent of B2B buyers saying they will have a favorable opinion of someone introduced via their professional network.

It's no surprise that internal LinkedIn data shows sales professionals with a high social selling index; a metric focused on how well salespeople develop their brand, focus on the right opportunities, interact with relevant material, and develop trustworthy relationships, with social sellers accessing all these essential benefits that give them the lead on their less socially-minded colleagues.

2. Your consumers are now interested in social purchasing,

What are social purchases? On its head, flip the idea of a social sale. Just as sales professionals can use social analysis techniques and social listening to find potential customers, those potential customers are also using social listening and social search to find potential vendors, analyze them online, and build an opinion about the vendor. It is the best fit before making the first contact with a sales professional.

In fact, CEB found that customers are, on average, 57 percent of the way through the purchasing process before they ever engage with a sales professional, and IDC found that as part of their buying process, 75 percent of B2B buyers and 84 percent of executives use social network contacts and details.

You're not showing up in the social sales research if you're not actively involved in social selling: that's a lot of possibly missed sales.

The good news is that 76% of buyers are prepared to have a social media conversation with potential providers, according to LinkedIn, and more than 62% of B2B buyers respond to salespeople who interact with them to share insights and opportunities related to their business. Even better, 92 percent of B2B customers are likely to connect with a sales professional who is a well-known industry thought leader. You can build credibility by regularly sharing insightful and meaningful social media material.

Beyond the initial transaction, bear in mind that 53% of consumer loyalty is driven by a salesperson's ability to provide unique insight, a skill that salespeople can initially demonstrate through their sharing of social media material, and then validate through their continuous social ties with past customers. Perhaps that is why Aberdeen's data reveals that social selling teams have a customer renewal rate seven percentage points higher than teams that have not implemented social selling instruments.

The biggest rivals are now using 3. Social selling

A record of 71% of all sales professionals and 90% of top salespeople are now using social selling software. The numbers are even higher among younger salespeople, with 78 percent of all millennial sales professionals using social sales tools, and 63 percent claiming those tools are essential or highly critical to their sales success. If you don't encourage your sales team to use social tools and equip them to do so, hiring top sales performers would be more difficult for you.

Also, brands are using social selling resources in just about every industry; whether it's Microsoft improving productivity by 38 percent by socially prospecting for leads for a new offering in cloud computing, the U.K. by using social selling to attract potential small and medium-sized business travel buyers, or the Vancouver Canucks using social selling to help with boosting of sales of hockey tickets, travel company Corporate Traveller gained £5.5 in new sales.

BEST PRATICES FOR SOCIAL SELLING

Let's look at some essential practices for implementing an effective social selling strategy to know what social selling is and why you should care.

1. Show up

Are you aware of what isn't very social? Robots. With automatic liking and commenting methods, you may be tempted to save time, but these do nothing to build relationships. They can do severe harm to your personal and professional brand. Yes, there are ways of integrating social bots into marketing and customer service, but nothing beats a real, living human when it comes to selling.

Therefore: Show up. Engage. Engage. Just be present. Just be yourself. Remember, building relationships is the point of social selling. The main objective is to make yourself seem more human, not less accessible.

Of course, since in your social selling efforts you'll hardly be alone, "show up" has another meaning, too. You need to make sure that when clients and prospects are searching for experts in your business, your profile shows up, so that they start identifying you as a pioneer in your field and a valuable touch.

To maximize the effect of your social selling plan, be sure to optimize your social media profiles across all networks. Look at your profiles from a client or prospect. Are they posing you as a trustworthy expert who has useful market-relevant insights? If not, do some editing to ensure that your profiles show you in the best possible light, and that all networks have a clear tone and message.

2. Listen to find strategic leads

On their social media, the clients and prospects exchange extremely useful details, essentially telling you exactly what they want and need. Everything you're meant to do is pay attention.

To track what individuals say about you, your company, your industry, and your rivals, use social lists and Hootsuite streams. Requests for recommendations and Watch for pain points, all of which provide you with natural opportunities to solve a problem.

Check their lists of supporters to see if you have any shared links, before reaching out to any of the leads you identify. If you do, ask for an introduction from your mutual contact. And make sure that your messages are personalized based on the wealth of knowledge people share on their professional social media accounts, such as a shared interest, or that you liked a blog post they shared in particular.

3. Provide value

There are no participation medals in social selling: if you're going to do it, you have to do it right. That means providing the right prospects with useful input at the right time.

It's essential not to get too "pitchy" when engaging with prospects and customers through social networks. Instead of simply praising your product or service's importance, your goal should be to provide useful information that can help you develop yourself as an expert in your field. Write posts that share valuable information, but don't fear sharing other people's related posts as well. Add a short statement of your own about how the material can be used in your particular field when sharing content from others.

It's definitely okay to mention your product or service in any of your social posts, but don't build sales pitches or presentations for your posts. In social selling, the aim is to build relationships that ultimately lead to a sale, not to make a sale on the first contact. That takes us to the last of our four social selling best practices ...

4. Create meaningful connections

Over time, stay in touch with your new social contacts. Pay attention to the content they post, and jump in with a like or a comment from time to time, to let them know that you have read and appreciated what they have to say.

Send a quick note of congratulations if a contact moves to a new position or business. Jump in with a meaningful answer, if you notice a contact asking for help or advice, even if it doesn't promote your product directly. Focus on how your contacts can be helped or make their lives easier. If you can develop yourself in your industry as their go-to guy, guess who they'll call when they're prepared to make a purchase?

HOW TO GET STARTED ON EACH PLATFORM WITH SOCIAL SALES

With the best practices above in mind, here are some specific tips on LinkedIn, Twitter, and Facebook to get started on social selling.

LinkedIn

As a professional social network, LinkedIn, particularly in the B2B space, is the most obvious social network for engaging in social sales. After all, when making purchasing decisions, 50 percent of B2B buyers use LinkedIn as a resource, and to position yourself as a player in those decisions, you need to be active on LinkedIn. Here are three key ways to start social selling using LinkedIn.

1. Establish your credibility

Ask for endorsements and suggestions from links that you have a good relationship with. These are posted on your profile and can help with new contacts to give you instant credibility. And make sure that your profile highlights expertise - rather than an employer - relevant to a potential customer. Highlight how you have helped previous clients accomplish their objectives.

2. Extend your network

Use the advanced search on LinkedIn to uncover possible new connections by leveraging existing network relationships.

An advisor at financial services firm Guardian Life picked up 35 referrals from just one customer using LinkedIn, according to Fortune. Since he began prospecting on social networks, the rep's business has more than doubled.

3. Get social in Groups

To start networking with peers and prospects, join LinkedIn Groups that are essential to your industry. To find new groups, use the search feature on your LinkedIn homepage, or choose from LinkedIn's suggestions for groups you might like.

You may also want to look into the Sales Navigator of LinkedIn, the professional social selling tool for the network.

Twitter

As a result of the ability to create Twitter Lists to monitor content from specific groups of people, Twitter is a great network for social listening. To get started with social selling on the network, here are three main Twitter lists you can use.

1. Current clients

To keep close tabs on your current customers and look for opportunities to respond to or like their Tweets, use this list to keep yourself on their radar.

However, do not overdo it, and make sure that your customer interactions are meaningful; only "like" Tweets that you like, and only comment when you have something useful to say. You might want to consider making this list public - unless you are in a super-secret industry - so that prospects can get a sense of what type of companies you are already serving.

2. Perspectives

You don't want to share this information with rivals while you classify possible future clients. Add them to a secret list, and do not let users know that you have classified them when the time is right to reach out to prospects. Keep a close eye on this list, too; just don't interact with the same sense of familiarity with current customers as you do. Keep a specific eye out for help requests or pain point statements, so as to reply with a helpful comment.

3. The Competitors

This list, again, ought to be private. Adding rivals to a personal list allows you to keep tabs on them without actually following them. For your social selling efforts, this competitive intelligence can help spark ideas.

Twitter chats can also be an essential part of your strategy for social selling. They allow you to establish yourself as an expert in the industry and serve as an essential strategy for prospecting. Join in or start your own on an existing chat that is relevant to your industry.

Facebook

When selling social media on Facebook, you have to be a bit more careful, as it is the most personal of the three social networks we're talking about in this post. Some people just don't want to mix business and fun on Facebook, so sending friend requests to company contacts or prospects might seem weird, rather than helpful. Instead, you may want to build a Facebook Business Page, then use these approaches to begin social sales.

1. Engaging with other firms

Via likes, comments, and shares, it is simple to reach out. Your outreach is likely to be reciprocated. Give insightful feedback and share useful material; this will place your Facebook page in front of a whole new audience, as your professional network expands and other organizations share and like your material in exchange.

2. Get involved with followers

Respond often to postings from followers. Try asking a question to spark debate amongst your followers on Facebook - posts that ask questions earn 100% more responses than normal text posts. This helps you enter the dialogue and engage directly with supporters, generating a sense of relationship and growing your expertise.

You might also ask followers about some of their most pressing issues, then build a report, whitepaper, or even just a post on Facebook to discuss their questions, including how your product or service can help.

Sales have always been about building partnerships, relationships, and reputation at the right moment, as well as offering the right answer to the right prospect. Selling socially doesn't change that. As a sales professional, it just gives you an additional suite of resources to integrate into your job, so that you can concentrate on the most efficient components of the sales process and leverage the advantages of established partnerships and interactions to create an enlarged network of customers who want to hear from you.

Creating Content More Easily With Artificial Intelligence

The need for fresh and individualized content, presto.

You know what? It is not that difficult, as you might think. To start, I have three awesome recipes for you here:

Recipe #7: Find astonishing content with AI

Ingredients: A tool like the MyCurator plugin for WordPress websites and a blog.

Method: How can I automate my reading list (Topic Sales Automation) to stay up to date? This was my question some years ago. At the end, I had set up the following system. In the core there is an AI plugin for WordPress called MyCurator. With MyCurator, you can easily find astonishing and relevant content on the web. First, you give the tool a list of relevant websites with an RSS feed of news (for example recode, TechCrunch, Harvard Business Review or any other publication of your niche). Then you add some keywords. The AI engine searches for this topics within the RSS flow and shows the findings on the training page. In the next four weeks, your task is to tell the engine which of the found articles is "good" and which is "bad". With this, you train the engine to get better and better. The good ones you can publish as a link recommendation on your blog, or you just get inspired to write a peace of content on your own. If you decide to publish it as a recommendation, you should mark it as "recommendation". When I did this, I put it on autopilot after five weeks. Since three years now, my blog with this automated recommendations is running and there was not a single mistake.

Difficulty: Intermediate.

Purpose: To get directly to relevant content.

Total time: 8 hours (without training time).

Recipe #8: Automated newsletter

Ingredients: Content from recipe #6, email marketing tool with RSS automation

Method: If you have the auto-generated content of recipe #6, this one is a no-brainer. Just set up your email marketing tool with an RSS automation on your blog´s category where all MyCurator recommendations go to. And then tell the email marketing tool to send out a digest of all new RSS entries once a week. I set this to Thursday. Every Thursday, my newsletter "DigitalSalesLab" is sent out to my list with new recommendations of blog posts and articles about sales automation. As I also get my own newsletter every Thursday, I open this email and get my own reading list. And nearly all Thursdays I think "Oh, this is so inspiring, every article sounds interesting!"

Difficulty: Beginner.

Purpose: Send out inspiring newsletter without hassle.

Total time: 30 minutes.

Recipe #9: Autopost evergreen content

Ingredients: Your own blog, relevant (to your buyer personas) social accounts, a service like Dlvr.it (or Hootsuite, Sprout Social, AgoraPulse).

Method: Oftentimes you have two kind of posts on your blog; the ones that target current topics and news, and then there are the one where you write about topics that will still be relevant some three or five years ahead. That's right, this is called evergreen content. And now you tell the social sharing service to pick the evergreen content (some services or WordPress plugins like Blog2social or Revive Old Posts let you do it randomly based on some variables such as category or age of the post). And you send it out again and again. Some services allow you to vary the text in the post linking to your blog post.

Difficulty: Beginner

Purpose: Getting seen in social. Social has to be compared rather with a TV news stream: For every minute you join the program, there are different pieces of content. Social is not like a wall newspaper where people are able to see all pieces of content in their moments of leisure. So if you want to get seen on social, you have to broadcast continuously all the time. As this is time-consuming, posting evergreen content is a good idea.

Total time: 2 hours.

We are in the middle of an explosion of material. In all places, and on all channels, customers expect to have personalized and meaningful experiences. An IDC survey reveals that 85 percent of advertising professionals feel under pressure to build capital and produce more campaigns faster. In reality, to help additional networks, over two-thirds of respondents generate over ten times more assets. The volume and related costs are driven by this increased degree of complexity.

When you think about anything involved in producing this kind of content at the breakneck speed needed for thousands or even millions of customers, doing it manually is no longer a choice. The State of Innovation in Business 2017 survey by Adobe reveals that 40% of creative people are still using AI in picture and design retouching. It can take your designers hours to search for the images alone, not counting the time needed to manipulate them, crop them, put them in different layouts, publish them in online catalogs and social media channels, and serve them at the right time to the right person. And for all that time, we haven't even discussed the cost or the expense of producing new properties from photoshoots.

You need the aid of artificial intelligence and machine learning, if you want to find and reuse assets more effectively, deliver new and personalized content on a scale, and get a better return on your investments.

Hashtag pro tip: Use hashtags wisely. Nearly all social channels allow unlimited numbers of hashtags. But LinkedIn for instance recommends using just three. So limit yourself to the most important ones. And which ones are the most important? The ones with the most followers and new content. Do a little research from time to time to evaluate the hashtags you use.

AI comprehension, machine learning, and deep learning

What does this mean, and how are they working? Here's the following short overview:

Artificial intelligence (AI) is computer science that studies how to make computers good for new kinds of tasks, particularly tasks that only human beings could do until recently.

Machine learning (ML) is a subfield of AI dedicated to developing programs that enhance their performance as more knowledge is provided to them, rather than requiring hand-programmed improved performance.

Deep learning is a set of ML methods loosely modeled on how brain neurons interact and respond to new knowledge. Deep-learning systems can identify objects in images when trained on very large quantities of data, recognize faces and facial expressions, describe an image's style or mood, and perform any number of other human-like tasks, all at high speed and on the scale.

Phil Gaughran, U.S. chief integration officer at McGarryBowen agency, made a bold statement during an Adobe Think Tank panel discussion at Advertising Week 2017: by 2022, he said, 80 percent of the advertising process will be automated," a threshold that will never be exceeded.

Invoking artificial intelligence's powers

Many of the mundane, repetitive tasks involved in producing content are automated by new progress in AI. And they are doing it extremely quickly, at high volume, and with high quality of production. If you release your designers from these time-consuming duties, they will be able to concentrate on the components of their jobs that require real, human creativity.

When used in customized workflows, AI has even more power, allowing you to more effectively find and manipulate assets and create complete campaigns with just a few clicks, while delivering highly personalized and engaging content in minutes. Yes, minutes.

The good news is that today there is a lot of this technology, and more exciting possibilities are close behind. The technology of today's artificial intelligence can help you do the following:

- Find and reuse current assets.

- Automate the manipulation of images and image creation.
- Creating and personalizing content on a scale.
- Understanding of content: In seconds, summon the perfect image.

Designers simply don't have time to tag every photoshoot with the hundreds of images uploaded. Even if they did, the keyword list would probably not be as comprehensive as it should be. But if a photo is not tagged, it's virtually impossible to find it by searching for thousands of images in an image bank. According to IDC, marketers report that one-third of marketing assets are unused or underused, with the average organization generating hundreds of new marketing assets every year. The probability of an image being repurposed is extremely small. Which means it'll also be your ROI.

Enter Auto Tag, an Adobe Sensei feature that automatically tags keyword images. Some of those keywords may be the beach, girl, dance, sundress, blue sky, white sand, or Aruba, using our example of a young girl on the beach.

The Auto Tag service is used in Adobe Experience Manager, Photo Search in Adobe Lightroom, and Visual Search in Adobe Stock to power the Smart Tags features. "Seeing the capabilities of auto-tagging is exciting," says Jonas Dahl, Adobe Experience Manager product manager. We did some manual search queries against the registry of a customer and showed the assets we were able to discover. We then used Smart Tagging and performed the same searches. The findings were considerably better and much more comprehensive this time. And within a fraction of the time.

Harnessing deep data and in-depth skills

With Adobe's broad domain experience in the artistic, marketing, and document segments, Adobe Sensei uses a centralized AI and machine-learning platform to leverage the vast volume of content and data assets of the organization, from high-resolution images to customer clicks.

Technology from Adobe Sensei has learned to recognize what is in a picture automatically. And the idea of the picture, including meaning, quality, and style, is not just an object like a car or a girl. This means that with the words "walking" and "slow," anyone could search for a picture. The search could result in a picture of an elderly man using a walker, since the technology made the connection between slow and walker. And it will tell you even more with the Adobe Sensei Auto-phrasing Service. It is possible to score each tag for prominence, so the computer knows the main and secondary artifacts. This helps the technology create a simple phrase or caption that explains the picture more accurately, such as an elderly man walking in a park with a walker.

You can train AI and machine-learning models to build your auto tags using the Adobe Sensei platform, customizing the models to learn and train on very specific parameters. This involves defining brand features such as your logo, so that brand expectations are adhered to by your designers. Or, you may train it to recognize your goods so that you can tag and recognize your true reach with photos on social media.

Amazing experiences: deeper insights from customers

Not only does custom auto-tagging improve the productivity of your squad, but it also opens the door to innovative new consumer experiences, such as image-based shopping. Now it's possible for a customer looking for a new couch to upload and shop for a photo of one they want based solely on the picture. As auto-tagging determines what is in the picture and finds the best matches, it's possible. Custom auto-tagging also enables you gain a deeper understanding of social media patterns in your audience and industry without relying on tags and text. If you operate a social media feed through Adobe Sensei, even if it is not listed or tagged, it will tag places where your brand is pictured, enabling you to see what is trending.

Computational imagination, editing at an incredible pace.

Once an image is found, editing it, cropping it, and creating the many different sizes and versions needed by your campaign can still take hours, unless you use AI. Let's look at some examples of Adobe Sensei's kinds of services and how they can have more engaging customer interactions, more efficiencies, and higher ROI.

With Deep Cutout. Save money on photo shoots by repurposing and hyper-personalizing existing photos. Your designers can automatically delete the background of an image and replace it with one that matches your brand's rules, such as a white background for all web images, or they will soon be able to mask an area like a highway and see what it looks like with a river, neighborhood, or other backdrops in just a few clicks, totally reinventing the picture in seconds.

Auto Harvest. Free. Time spent cropping and sizing images eats into valuable design cycles for distinct aspect ratios. But now, by training the auto-crop model to crop images by your brand guidelines, you can automate this process. For example, a shoe manufacturer might have rules that specify that only the shoe be displayed, so all images can be cropped accordingly.

Quality of image. You can train the API on image aesthetics to pick the best image automatically and reject anything below a certain level. Validation of quality may be focused on exposure, concentration, the balance of color, field depth, and more. This saves precious time by removing lower-quality images automatically.

Use the magic of custom workflows

Your team will be able to produce hundreds or thousands of campaign assets in no time, by using the capabilities mentioned above. Incredible time savings will result even from only one of these capabilities, but the rate at which you can create content gets faster and faster as you add them together. The technology's real power and cost savings come from creating custom workflows that allow you to scan, mask, crop, and publish in minutes.

About the author

With more than 20 years of experience, Tim Cortinovis is a proven expert on sales and marketing automation. *How can I set sales and marketing on autopilot, even as a SME?* This is his guiding principle. He has inspired thousands of entrepreneurs and professionals to digitise and automate customer interaction.

Tim helps companies face the fast-paced customer expectations by leveraging smart automation techniques, and gives answers to the urgent question of how to involve teams heading to the future.

Tim is an entrepreneur and global keynote speaker. Clients and audiences love his energetic way of storytelling and his innovative examples. He speaks about how we can use AI and automation in our current business models and, how we inspire our teams to follow us. Before graduating in language and communications, he worked as a TV news anchorman and also published a novel and a podcast. When he is not spending time with his family, he can be found (fast) sailing.

At the age of 16 he built up his first AI chatbot. Tim is a graduate of university studies in language and literature. When he is not with his family he can be found sailing (dinghy and offshore).

LinkedIn: Tim Cortinovis

Web: Cortinovis.de

Twitter: @timcortinovis

Tim is available for speaking engagements as well as consulting.

Gratitude

This book would not have been possible without the help of my speaker friends and my community. To all of you: Thank you soooo much for your input and inspiration!

Special thanks to: Oliver Leisse, Jason Campbell, Ben Harmanus, Carmen Hentschel, Sönke Rohde, Martin Klapheck, Thomas Paul, Raphaël Muschalla, Sophie Hundertmark, Jens Reinhard and James Wedmore.

Notes

Used and useful books and resources (in order of appearance)

Reid Hoffmann: *Blitzscaling: The Lightning-Fast Path to Building Massively Valuable Companies.* Penguin Random House.

Marketing automation software market - growth, trends, forecasts (2020 - 2025). Url: https://www.mordorintelligence.com/industry-reports/global-marketing-automation-software-market-industry

DemandGenReport. URL: https://www.demandgenreport.com/

Driving impact at scale from automation and AI. A study by McKinsey. URL: https://www.mckinsey.com/~/media/McKinsey/Business%20Functions/McKinsey%20Digital/Our%20Insights/Driving%20impact%20at%20scale%20from%20automation%20and%20AI/Driving-impact-at-scale-from-automation-and-AI.ashx

Marketing Automation & Your CRM. URL: https://www.pardot.com/blog/marketing-automation-crm-infographic/

The Ultimate Marketing Automation statistics overview. URL: https://www.emailmonday.com/marketing-automation-statistics-overview/

SMT's State of Marketing Automation Survey 2019 - Part 1: Current State of Automation. URL: https://www.socialmediatoday.com/news/smts-state-of-marketing-automation-survey-2019-part-1-current-state-of/551755/

Marketing Automation Trends for Success. URL: https://www.threedeepmarketing.com/media/1598/three-deep-marketing-automation-trends-for-success-final.pdf

McKinsey Global Institute. Skill shift: Automation and the future of the workforce. URL: https://www.mckinsey.com/featured-insights/future-of-work/skill-shift-automation-and-the-future-of-the-workforce

Social Selling: What it is, Why You Should Care, and How to Do It Right. URL: https://blog.hootsuite.com/what-is-social-selling/

Schafter, Cole: "9 Social Media Automation Tools That Will Make Your Job Easier". URL https://blog.hootsuite.com/social-media-automation/.

Spread the word

If you found this book useful, please share it with your friends and community, as a way of encouraging your peers to save time and get into their heroine or hero roles again. There are a number of easy ways to do this:

1. Write an Amazon review of the book.
2. Gift this book to a friend or colleague who needs to read it.
3. Write a blog post about building your sales and marketing automations (#roboticsales).
4. Host a #roboticsales-themed brown bag lunch party at your company, and talk about how your teams can support each other's automation efforts.